# IBN KHALDUN
## EDUCATION, HISTORY & SOCIETY

*To Hannah Shafi*

# IBN KHALDUN
## EDUCATION, HISTORY & SOCIETY

### Shamim Miah

BEACON BOOKS

Published in the UK by Beacon Books and Media Ltd
Earl Business Centre, Dowry Street, Oldham, OL8 2PF, UK.

www.beaconbooks.net

ISBN: 978-1-915025-38-8 Paperback
ISBN: 978-1-915025-39-5 Hardback
ISBN: 978-1-915025-40-1 eBook

Cataloging-in-Publication record for this book is available from the British Library

Cover design by Raees Mahmood Khan

# Contents

**Chapter 4**
**Ibn Khaldun, *Asabiyya* and the Rule of Four ............ 85**

# *Acknowledgments*

It takes more than the author to write a book—indeed, it is only made possible with the help of others. Thus, it's my duty and obligation to extend my gratitude and appreciation for the help and support I have received from students, family, friends, and teachers.

I have been blessed to have inquisitive PhD students that have shaped the direction of this book over numerous discussions over coffee. In particular I would like to thank Muzaffer Can-Dilek, Muhammad Zakir, Muhammad Farooqui and Bilal Nazir. I would like to thank the team at the Centre of Postnormal Policy and Futures Studies, especially Jordi Serra Del Pina, Chris Jones, Liam Mayo and Scott Jordan. My deepest appreciation is extended to Ziauddin Sardar.

This project has taken many years to come to fruition. It started as a conversation with Jamil Chishti on the way back from the BRAIS conference at The University of Chester in 2017. However, I was forced to take short breaks to complete other writing projects which resulted in the publication date being delayed several times. I am grateful to Jamil for his patience and continued interest in this book. I would also like to thank Siema Rafiq, the editor at Beacon Books, for her diligent scholarship and helpful comments on the various drafts.

# Foreword

*Anwar Ibrahim*

Ibn Khaldun's life, thought and work has inspired a vast array of thinking that informs our world today. Many volumes have been written on his scholarly output and intellectual pursuits. 'If you tried to read everything that has been written about Ibn Khaldun,' says Robert Irwin, the erudite British historian, 'you would die before you could finish the job.' So, Irwin goes on to ask, why should he pen yet another biography, especially when Ibn Khaldun himself had noted that there were already too many books to be read in his own time? Yet, as the existence of Irwin's book attests, he did not stop writing and we should be glad he did not.

Shamim Miah's book is not only a valuable addition to the literature on Ibn Khaldun—whose full name was Wali al-Din 'Abd al-Rahman Ibn Khaldun—but provides new insights into his thought on education and society. It is focused on showing the relevance of his intellectual discourse in our turbulent and complex postnormal times.

As the Muslim world's greatest historiographer, Ibn Khaldun's life can and has been intricately tied to his magnum opus, the *Muqaddimah*. But his thought was not just one monumental tome. He was also a man living during a time when the world was in the grip of a plague, a man who played a role in the courts of Andalusian and North African rulers, who walked across North Africa (an almost unimaginable task), and who crossed words with the great conqueror Tamerlane. It should come as no surprise that the words written about him surpass the not insignificant number of words he wrote during his short time on this Earth.

For Ibn Khaldun was not just a great scholar of the classical period. He was a polymath. Our packaged and highly categorised, fast-paced modern existence has not only diminished our appreciation for such a genius, but even consigned it to the realm of mythology and legend.

This is, of course, a myopic view of a great mind—an intellectual luminary. A polymath is not one who knows it all. It is not just about a well-rounded, multidisciplinary (even transdisciplinary) education, but about the relentless pursuit of a well-rounded, multifaceted life.

Our contemporary world has tricked us into thinking that such a pursuit is as futile as it is utopian. Two facets lead us to believe such noble goals are hopeless. First, the claim of postmodernism that there are no universals. This has ushered us into a field of relativeness filled with the thistles and weeds of political correctness, cancel culture, and a tragic waste of intellectual effort. The second comes by way of our 24/7, instantaneous updates and notifications. The internet of things, apps, social media, and the nonstop inundation with information presented on the stage set by post-truth and the death of expertise. Indeed, who can know it all? Is that not, after all, subjective? Why would one even try when one has Google, and now ChatGPT, and the mushrooming of enhanced rival modalities to heed every beck and call? The only option is to specialise, yet the stakes are insurmountable. Every expert is only one overlooked data set or unread paper from instant ruin when an absurd form of justice is served up cold by internet mob-mentality.

Worst yet, most of our specialisations were set in stone in a bygone era and not only their purpose, but their epistemologies, are outdated. This can be quite treacherous for the future of knowledge creation. And this, granted largely Western, obsession with categories and the specific takes its origins in the Ancient Greek world, where we find a time-loved metaphor for our dilemma—the fox and the hedgehog. In the seventh century BCE, the Ancient Greek lyrical poet Archilochus wrote that 'a fox knows many things, but a hedgehog knows one big thing'. While Archilochus's fable would launch a dichotomy between two approaches to formation, it would not be until the twentieth century, when the Russian-British philosopher Isaiah Berlin took on the metaphor, that a new appreciation would be put forward concerning this code for thinkers.

In his aptly titled 1953 essay, 'The Hedgehog and the Fox', Berlin draws up a list of hedgehog and fox thinkers throughout history. Yet, he scratches his head when trying to fit Leo Tolstoy into this dichotomy. To say he did not neatly fit into one list or the other is a vast understatement. As Berlin writes, 'the question does not, somehow, seem wholly appropriate; it seems to breed more darkness than it dispels.' Almost seventy years later, it looks like the hedgehog has largely won the day and the idea of a 'fox' is equated to that of a 'fool', or at least one who is directionless and not fitting the model of success in our contemporary neoliberal capitalist societies. Our young minds are forced into antiquated siloed disciplines, and the intellectual is confined to the ivory tower with the sentence of 'publish or perish' as the world moves on without them. Perhaps those who have read Berlin's analysis simply consider Tolstoy as a historical anomaly. But it is critical to understand that Berlin has happened upon a serious contradiction in a fundamental philosophical conception. And as we pull at the strands of this contradiction, it becomes clear that this dichotomy is a needless categorisation. In our contemporary state, where even a global pandemic cannot make us forget how much we need each other, we need to appreciate more critically such anomalies and those who lay bare the cracks in our foundations.

Ibn Khaldun is a mind I think Berlin would have a similar issue with categorising. But, Ibn Khaldun also plays both the role of Tolstoy and Berlin, in that during his time, he too spotted a contradiction in need of reflection.

In his criticism and revision, he invented the field of historiography, forever changing how historians conduct their business. While it is essential that we carry forward our stories, the critical edge of scholarly scrutiny and questioning makes sure we carry forward truth, and that the lessons, morals, and values transmitted do not become adulterated by bias or misunderstanding. Otherwise, history remains at the discretion of the victor. Recalling T.S. Eliot's reminder that history can incarcerate as much as it can liberate, the history of my country and my role in it could so easily have been written in the lies and fears that had me spending over a decade of my life in prison. So, in a way, Ibn Khaldun sought to prepare us for the world he could not have even begun to imagine.

Simultaneously, he broke the mould in international relations, law, sociology, economics, the written word, and so much more. Ask ten friends what Ibn Khaldun's greatest intellectual contributions were and you'll get as many answers, if not more! He was much more than just a scholar; he was a citizen who did his duty in the many places he made his home, and a diplomat who went toe-to-toe with tyrants.

Few have left such a mark on their world and even though he existed outside of the dates most reserve for the 'Islamic Golden Age', he is often included within that prestigious pantheon of thinkers. And while I think he would have the humility to confirm that he did not in fact know everything there was to know during his lifetime, his influence knew no bounds. He embodied the Muslim call to read and to learn and discover all the mysteries of our world. Despite the growth in the study of Ibn Khaldun in the West, his contributions to the field of social sciences is often limited to the academic community. Shamim Miah's introductory book brings the works of Ibn Khaldun to a much broader audience by drawing upon the *Muqaddimah* to provide insights into his ideas on education, sociology and history. I hope that countless other studies on his life and works will fill bookshelves, unpacking the wisdom he left behind.

We are fortunate here to hold yet another entry point into the genius and boundless intellectual immensity of Ibn

Khaldun. But I beckon you to read on. Read everything you can get your hands on. Read the primary sources and read how different people came to find Ibn Khaldun, just as you yourself found him. Build upon this great discourse and add your contribution. And in doing so, transcend the inane barriers society puts on thought and knowledge creation. The return of the Islamic Golden Age that many of us so desperately pray for comes in living our traditions and doing as we were made to do—to learn, to know, and to seek the truth. And our polymaths of history have thus far led the way. Now we need a plural community that fosters the creation of future polymaths so that our dreams for a better tomorrow can be built and come to pass. In our postnormal times, the polymath will be essential in helping us navigate the uncertainty and ignorance that plagues our transitions ahead.

The polymath bridges distant lands, civilisations, and histories. From a sociologist in Oldham to a kampong boy in Malaysia, we can all come to Ibn Khaldun from a variety of roads and be reminded that the world is an ever-changing place and that we have to power in the direction that change takes us.

Anwar Ibrahim
April 2023

# *Introduction*

He created us from the earth as living, breathing creatures. He made us settle on it as races and nations. From it, He provided sustenance and provisions for us.

The wombs of our mothers and houses are our abode. Sustenance and food keep us alive. Time wears us out. Our lives: final terms the dates of which have been fixed for us in the book (of destiny), claim us.

But He lasts and persists. He is the Living One who does not die.

Ibn Khaldun, Muqaddimah

Ibn Khaldun—the famous historian, sociologist and jurist—is a popular name within the Muslim world. His face appears on banknotes in the country of his birth, Tunisia, and his legacy is commemorated through postage stamps in Egypt, the country of his death. But Ibn Khaldun's name is not confined to North Africa; he is widely acknowledged throughout the Muslim world with countless universities, schools, streets and buildings named in his honour. In the West, his name is associated with the chair of Islamic studies at the American University, Washington, DC and his contribution to sociology is acknowledged within A-Level sociology textbooks in the United Kingdom. Not only has Ibn Khaldun influenced contemporary historians, sociologists and intellectuals throughout Europe and the US, but his ideas on economics have been quoted by the former Prime Minister of Britain, Boris Johnson, and the former President of the United States, Ronald Reagan.

Ibn Khaldun was born in 1332 and was an active political advisor, scholar and jurist at a time when classical Islamic civilisation had passed its zenith. Despite this, Ibn Khaldun would in many respects embody and continue the legacy of learning and scholarship of classical Islam. Like his intellectual predecessors, he would go on to leave a lasting influence on a range of academic disciplines including history, religion, and politics. At the same time, he developed new disciplines, such as sociology.

Ibn Khaldun was born at a time when the study of biographies was an established discipline. Most people consider biographies a modern literary phenomenon. In fact, during the classical Muslim period, it was an established science called the *Tabaqat*. Indeed, for Ibn Khaldun, the study of the *Tabaqat* served an important feature in assessing the nature of *asabiyya,* or group solidarity. Thus, it was not surprising that Ibn Khaldun wrote his own biography titled, *Al-Ta'rif bi Ibn Khaldun wa rihalatihi sharqan wa gharbub* (Presenting Ibn Khaldun and His Journey East and West), which gives a

2

detailed account of his life, philosophy and politics. Sadly, there are no translations of *Al-Ta'rif bi Ibn Khaldun* in English; however, there is a partial French translation by Abdesselam Cheddadi, titled *Le Voyage d'Occident et d'Orient* (Paris, 1980). Ibn Khaldun's *Al-Ta'rif* provides helpful insights into his life and works, but has been criticised by many for omitting detailed information on his career. For example, the *Al-Ta'rif* does not mention his early writings, such as his commentary of the *Qasidat al-Burdah* by Imam Al-Busiri (d.1294), or his abridged works on the philosopher and polymath Al-Razi (d.925) and Ibn Rushd (d.1198). To gain an appreciation of the complete works of Ibn Khaldun, historians have consulted wider related sources, including the writings of his friend and poet, Ibn al-Khatib (d.1374), the famous Andalusian polymath who published several insightful works on medicine, poetry, philosophy, and history. As a close friend and contemporary of Ibn Khaldun, he was able to provide further insights into his writings. This is captured by the following observation:

> [Ibn Khaldun] wrote an original commentary on the *Burdah*, in which he showed his wide ability, his understanding of many things and his great knowledge. He abridged a good deal of the books of Averroes [Ibn Rushed]. He put together a useful composition on logic for the Sultan, in the days when he studied the intellectual disciplines. He abridged the *Muhassal* of Imam Fakhr-ad-din ar-Razi. At the time of writing, he has begun to write a commentary on a *rajaz* poem, composed on the principles of jurisprudence. What he has (done) already is so perfect that it cannot be surpassed.
>
> (Rosenthal 1958, Vol.1: xliv).

3

Ibn Khaldun was born into a politically influential family in Seville during the Muslim rule of Andalusia. According to his biography, his family lineage can be traced back to Hadhramaut in Yemen. The Khaldun family enjoyed intellectual and political fame in Andalusia, which came to a dramatic end when the city of Seville was defeated by the advancing Christian army in 1230. As a result, the family took political refuge in Tunisia under the Hafsid Dynasty where Ibn Khaldun was born in the city of Tunis. The political connections of Ibn Khaldun's family would play a significant role in the development of his future career as an advisor to several leading Muslim rulers, during a tumultuous period in North Africa with political rivalries between competing Muslim dynasties, each seeking to control the crucial gold and salt trade routes (Lacoste 1984:17–18).

Ibn Khaldun's life is connected with his seminal book, the *Muqaddimah* (Introduction or Prolegomena). The *Muqaddimah* was not always a standalone text; in fact, the famous work consists of a brief introduction (fifty-three pages in the English translation) and Book 1 of his monumental seven-volume text on the universal *Book of History,* or to give it its correct title, *Kitab al-Ibar wa-diwan al-mubtada wa-l-khabr fi ayyam al-arab wa-l-ajam wa-l barbar* (Book of Examples and the Collection of Origins of the History of the Arabs and Berbers). However, throughout the lifespan of Ibn Khaldun the original Introduction and Book 1 became an independent book, which came to be known as the *Muqaddimah*. Ibn Khaldun himself, whilst teaching this text in Egypt during the latter part of his life, referred to the Introduction and Book 1 as the *Muqaddimah*. Rosenthal (2005) writes in the introduction to his translation of the *Muqaddimah* that this seminal text can be,

> regarded as the earliest attempt made by any historian to discover a pattern in the changes that occur in man's political and social organization. Rational in its approach, analytical in its method, encyclopaedic in detail, it represents an almost complete departure from traditional historiography, discarding conventional concepts and clichés and seeking, beyond the mere chronicle of events, an explanation—and hence a philosophy of history.
>
> (Ibn Khaldun 2005:xxxix)

Ibn Khaldun's analytical method is grounded upon an inter-disciplinary approach. His eclectic approach draws upon a range of disciplines, including the natural sciences, geography, history, philosophy, Islamic studies, linguistics, and philosophy. Unlike his predecessors, such as Ibn Rushd (d.1198) and Ibn Sina (d.1037), he was not only interested in high logic and philosophical theory, but was equally motivated by the desire to understand and explain human interaction. The writing style of the *Muqaddimah* is aimed at the scholarly community and not the general masses. Scholars have noted how the cultural speech and academic discourse used in the *Muqaddimah* reflects academic discussions used by his contemporaries throughout the Muslim world. In fact, the language resembles the formal speech of a university lecturer, addressing an audience through a structured presentation. A significant section of the *Muqaddimah* echoes the corpus of Muslim literature that is influenced by a style which aims to fulfil intellectual curiosity.

The writing style, together with the repetitive nature of the *Muqaddimah*, has attracted some criticism throughout the years. It is often remarked how the text could be 'reduced to about half its size and would then be a much more readable work, especially to readers unable to savour the richness of the original language or the unwillingness to follow all the nuances and subtle variations in the workings of a great scholarly mind' (Rosenthal, 1958, Vol.1: lxix). Ibn Khaldun wrote the *Muqaddimah* in a secluded space in Qal'at ibn Salamah (Algeria) without the aid of a library. In fact, a significant section of his works were based upon memory, including quotations of various books by Ibn Arabi, Al-Masudi, etc. For some, this is a huge testament to the remarkable ability of classical scholars to memorise not only the Qur'an but a plethora of key works. For others, this reflects one of the shortcomings of the *Muqaddimah*, by allowing various misquotations and incorrect source references to creep into the text (see Rosenthal, 1958, pp. lxix–lxxi). Despite this, Ibn Khaldun's *Muqadimmah* is considered a masterpiece, not because of the rational and analytical manner through which the author viewed human history and society, but because he was the first to depart from the traditional method, which viewed history as a set of predictable clichés and events predicated upon exaggerated superstitions. For Ibn Khaldun, the secret to understanding history lies beyond the chronicles of dates and events to a much broader explanation of the philosophy underpinning it.

This book does not intend to add anything new to the existing study of Khaldunian scholarship; instead, it aims to provide an introduction that will give students and the general reader an insight into the dynamic life and work of Ibn Khaldun. It was in part an outcome of my own frustrations during my doctoral studies in trying to locate an introductory text that would function as a stepping-stone to his more serious academic works. Furthermore, this book intends to focus on a hitherto neglected area of Ibn Khaldun studies, as it concentrates on three key areas, namely: epistemology (theory of knowledge), education (especially pedagogy), politics and sociology (or theory of society).

The first chapter of this book aims to provide a broad socio-political landscape of Ibn Khaldun's life. It introduces the reader to the endless political dramas of the fourteenth century which shaped the history and society of North Africa. It further discusses the legacies of two leading Islamic empires, namely the Almoravid and Almohad dynasties, which influenced Ibn Khaldun's theory of society and politics. The replacement of the Almoravid dynasty by the Almohads, together with the inevitable decline of the latter's political rule, gave way to three competing Muslim dynasties in the Maghreb which would struggle for control throughout Ibn Khaldun's own life. The Hafsid dynasty would rule from Iraqiya, which is situated in present-day western Libya and Tunisia, while the Marinid Dynasty ruled from Morocco. Finally, the Zayyad dynasty ruled central Maghreb from the central North African city of Tlemcen (Fromherz, 2011).

Chapter Two starts with a discussion on the concept of knowledge within classical Islam before highlighting Ibn Khaldun's own approach to classification of knowledge. It shows how Ibn Khaldun recognised the importance of *traditional sciences* as founded within the study of Qur'an,

Hadith, theology, jurisprudence, and the Arabic language. He further recognised the significance of *philosophical* or *intellectual sciences*, such as logic, physics, metaphysics, and mathematics.

Chapter Three considers Ibn Khaldun's views on schooling, education, and pedagogy. Some of the key themes of epistemology of knowledge are further picked up here by looking at Ibn Khaldun's approaches to the study of history, including his view of history as an 'extraordinary science', which offered a radical shift from conventional ways of studying it. The Khaldunian approach is sceptical of presenting history as a chronology of dates and events. Instead, it recognises the importance of critically assessing historical records with the aim of discovering patterns that occur within society.

The concluding chapter brings together Ibn Khaldun's sociological theory of *asabiyya* as a way of explaining the rise and fall of civilisations and political dynasties. For Ibn Khaldun, history acts as a constant present; societal norms and political ideas are shaped by history, which both inform the present and shape the future. Ibn Khaldun, with his tools of 'historical thinking' and sociological imagination, was able to record how *asabiyya* was the driving force of history, and fundamentally determined the rise and fall of dynasties (Fromherz, 2010). To examine this rise and fall Ibn Khaldun developed his *cyclical theory*: the cycle of groups from rural areas with strong group solidarity replacing the existing weaker groups of the cities repeats itself every four generations.

Ibn Khaldun was a mature person with decades of political and scholarly activity behind him—he was forty-five years of age when he wrote the *Muqaddimah*. In true testament to

8

his scholarship and brilliance, he managed to complete the *Muqaddimah* in less than five months (Enan 1993:52). As with any major text, it went through several revisions before it was published. Once this monumental work was complete, Ibn Khaldun wrote the following words of poetry in recognition of the patronage and support given by Sultan Abu-al Abbas (discussed further in Chapter 1). It began with the following:

> Here in the histories of time and people
>> Are lessons the morals of which are followed by the just.
>
> I summarised all the books of the ancients
>> And recorded what they omitted.
>
> I smoothed the methods of expression
>> As if they submitted to my will.
>
> I dedicate it, a glory, to your realm, which shines, and is the object of pride.
>> I swear that I did not exaggerate
>
> A bit; exaggeration is hateful to me.
>
> (Cited in Enan 1993:56)

# Chapter 1

# *Ibn Khaldun:*
# *Socio-Political Landscape*

**D**eciding the starting point of Ibn Khaldun's biography is very difficult. Does one start with his ideas on history, sociology, or politics? Or is it helpful to start with his formative years of family, education and historical context? If historical context is an ideal starting point, this then raises a further question of how far back in history does one begin?

This chapter aims to provide the reader with a detailed outline of Ibn Khaldun's career. In short, there are three important themes arising from the brief biographical outline of Ibn Khaldun's life. (A summary is provided in Table 1 at the end of this chapter.)

First, Ibn Khaldun's life was fundamentally shaped by the political drama of North Africa, especially relating to the Hafsid dynasty and the Marinid sultanate, two competing political forces during his lifetime. In order to make sense of the Hafsid dynasty it is critical to understand the two major dynasties that ruled North Africa before Ibn Khaldun's time, namely, the Almoravid dynasty, which was defeated by the Almohads in 1147. The Hafsids replaced the Almohads in 1229, continuing the Almohad theo-political governance developed by their founder Ibn Tumart (d.1130). Second, the history of North Africa was deeply connected with Ibn Khaldun's own roots. Ibn Khaldun came from an influential aristocratic* family, tracing his lineage through Yemen, Andalusia and North Africa, and Ibn Khaldun's grandfather worked under the Hafsids. Given Ibn Khaldun's intimate knowledge of the dynamics of political rule, it is unsurprising that his career seems to be motivated by political expediency; this is clear from his shifting alliances with competing dynastic rulers. Finally, during Ibn Khaldun's later years, he settles down and spends significant time in Egypt completing his magnum opus, whilst carrying out teaching duties and administrating justice through his role as a Maliki judge.

## Ibn Khaldun's Early Family History

To comprehend the significance of Ibn Khaldun's lineage, it is crucial to understand the early history of Muslim Spain, which began with the weakening presence of the Visigoths and the expansion of the Umayyad dynasty. The conquest of Spain was made possible by the Umayyad military commander Tariq ibn Ziyad (d.720), who was able to cross the Straits of Gibraltar from the North African coasts before consolidating his troops on the Rock of Gibraltar, or Jabel Tariq, from which it derives its name. During the early eighth century, the Khaldun family migrated to Carmona, in the province of Seville in Andalusia (Al-Andalus). Al-Andalus or 'Muslim Spain' is located in the southern part of Spain, which was under Muslim rule from 711–1492 (Jayyusi, 1994). Muslim Spain would continue to provide rich contributions to art, philosophy, science and medicine. This legacy would be closely associated with the triangle of three great cities: Cordoba, Seville and Granada. Muslims in Spain would leave behind a complex, civilised and highly cultivated society providing a beacon for future societies. The above three cities would play a key role in shaping knowledge and culture: philosophy and theology through the Great Mosque in the city of Cordoba, the irrigated fountains and eloquent poetry of Granada, and the breathtaking art and architecture of Seville.

Muslim Spain would also play a critical role in transmitting, editing, commenting on and developing Greek philosophy throughout Europe. In doing so, they would go on to develop a culture of tolerance between Muslims, Christians and Jews. In addition to this, the above three majestic cities were considered by many to be the 'ornament of the world' (Mecocal, 2003). Cordoba was the intellectual hub for learning, given its famous libraries and bookshops. According to the philosopher and genealogist Ibn Hazm (d.1063), the ruler Hakim II, who was also a distinguished historian, established twenty-seven free schools and established a library of over 400,000 volumes. For al-Qashandi, the libraries of Cordoba were ranked alongside other great libraries of the Muslim world, including the Abbasids in Baghdad and that of the Fatimids in Cairo (Hillenbrand, 1994). More significantly, Ibn Said notes how:

> Cordoba held more books than any other city in Andalus, and its inhabitants were the most enthusiastic in caring for their libraries; such as collections were regarded as symbols of status and social leadership. Men who had no knowledge whatsoever would make it their business to have a library in their homes; they would be selective in the acquisitions, so that they might boast of possessing unique copies in the handwriting of a particular calligrapher.
>
> (Hillenbrand 1994:120)

The Khaldun family can trace their lineage to Hadramaut, Yemen. This claim of Arab genealogy has long been criticised and its authenticity questioned by a number of biographers of Ibn Khaldun. They point to the fact that it was politically expedient at the time to display Arab roots. It was considered a coveted honour, considering their socio-political dominance and influence in Andalusia (Enan, 1993: 4–5). Some have even argued that Ibn Khaldun may have had Berber and/ or Spanish heritage (Rosenthal, 1958:xxxiv), a claim which is attributed to the Swedish scholar, Count Jacob Graberg of Hemso (Gotland), but rejected by several Khaldunian specialists (Schmidt, 1930:35). Graberg travelled to Morocco in 1816 and remained there for six years in search of Ibn Khaldun's handwritten copy of the *Muqaddimah*. Moreover, it will be made clear throughout this book that Ibn Khaldun's Andalusian influence would play a central role in his intellectual and political development.

Despite the differences of opinion relating to his lineage, one thing is for sure: Ibn Khaldun's family takes a prominent role in the history of Islam in Al-Andalus, after one of his family members played a pivotal role in helping the Yemenite troops to settle in Carmona, where the Banu Khaldun was established (Rosenthal, 1958). By the early eighth century, the Banu Khaldun moved to Seville, and it wasn't long until the Khaldun name was forever associated with the city of Seville. During the late ninth century, the Banu Khaldun was further consolidated after one of Ibn Khaldun's ancestors (Kurayb Ibn Khaldun) revolted against the Umayyad *amir* to establish an independent autonomous principality in Seville. Along with other prominent and powerful families, they played a salient role in the political activities of the city, until their fateful demise following the rise of Christian rule under King Ferdinand III of Castile. The Banu Khaldun, given their political connections with the Hafsids (see below), were able to leave Seville and make the journey to northwest Africa before the end of the infamous siege of Seville in 1248.

## North African Politics: Almoravids, Almohads and the Hafsids

To gain an understanding of Ibn Khaldun's life, it is critical to navigate the complex political drama of North Africa, especially relating to the rise and fall of dynastic rule. The key players in the political life of Ibn Khaldun were the Hafsid dynasty and its rival, the Marinid Sultanate. To fully appreciate this schism, one must first appreciate the preceding dynasties that ruled North Africa; namely, the Almoravids and the Almohads. The disintegration of Umayyad rule, marked by the fall of Toledo in 1085, gave rise to the subsequent rule of two Berber Empires: the Almoravids (or Al-Murabitun) followed

15

by the Almohads. The Almoravids were Berbers from the Sanhaja tribe, while the Almohads (or al-Muwahhidun) were descendants of the Masmuda tribe. As indicated below, both tribes had a great deal in common:

> There are various similarities between the Almohad and Almoravid empires. Both came into existence in north-west Africa, and then later included al-Andalus in their territories. Both were ruled by a Berber tribesman. Both were in their origin religious movements, or perhaps rather had a religious basis. It was only natural, of course, that the Berbers, who supported the Almohads, should be the centuries-old of those who supported the Almoravids. The latter were nomads of the group of tribes known as Sanhaja, whereas the former were mountaineers from the Atlas belonging to the Masmuda.
>
> (Watt and Cachia 1996:103)

The Almoravids began ruling circa 1039 with Abdullah ibn Yasin (d.1059), a Maliki Muslim theologian who played a dominant role in the history and politics of the region by successfully defeating a range of Christian armies, especially in the pivotal Battle of Sagrajas during the late eleventh century. The Almoravids were famous for their fortified buildings, or *Ribat*, which can still be seen in places such as Monastir, Tunisia. These *Ribats* were physical defence structures that were protected by military volunteers, or Murabitun. The Murabitun were warrior-Sufis, known for their piety and equally famous for their skill in combat. The Almoravids were to revive Islam throughout the region, whilst defending against the encroachment of Christian rule in the south of Spain.

The Almohads ruled most of North Africa from 1147–1229 and replaced the Almoravid dynasty. The Almohads constituted mainly of Berber (sometimes referred to as Amazigh) Muslims, a distinctive indigenous ethnic group from North and West Africa with their own language and culture. They had a rich and complex civilisation before the arrival of Arab armies. Several academics have pointed out the historical tensions between the Berbers and the Arabs. For example, it is argued that 'the Berbers took part in the conquest of Andalusia and bore the greatest burden, while the Arabs alone enjoyed authority and rule. This antagonism lasted very long until the Arab racial predominance declined, and the Berbers began to dominate in the early part of the fifth century [AH]' (Enan, 1993:4).

The Almohad dynasty was founded by Ibn Tumart (c.1080–1130), a Muslim Berber, renowned religious scholar and political leader. Ibn Tumart travelled widely throughout the Muslim world in pursuit of sacred knowledge; it is even claimed that he studied under the famous theologian, al-Ghazali (d.1111). Considering his newly found inspirations arising from travels and study, Ibn Tumart believed that the Almoravids were too relaxed and soft in their approach to establish Islam as a complete and comprehensive way of life. Thus, it was not surprising to see the Almohads, a movement which put greater emphasis on *tawhid*, or unity of Allah, challenge the political order of the Almoravids. The movement gained momentum as they put greater emphasis on the Qur'an, Hadith and the theology of Imam al-Ashari (d.936). In fact, Ibn Tumart had very little tolerance of Berber customs and practices, which he felt did not conform to Islamic principles.

However, it would be Ibn Tumart's successor, Caliph Abd al-Mumin, who would eventually put an end to the Almoravid dynasty in 1147.

The Almohads governed most of North Africa from their capital Marrakech, Morocco, and expanded their reach to include Al-Andalus by 1172. Under the Almohad rule of Muslim Spain, there were several significant changes in the social and religious fabric of society. For example, the Almohads favoured the Ash'ari school of Islamic theology over the Zahiri school, which was the dominant school supported by the Almoravids. Zahirite theology was developed by Muslim theologian Dawud al-Zahiri (d.884), who put greater emphasis on the outward (or *zahiri*) meanings of expressions in the Qur'an and hadith. The Almohads also maintained a different political stance regarding the status of non-Muslims; under the Almoravids both Christians and Jews were given *dhimmi* status (i.e. they were allowed to practise their religion providing the payment of tax (*jizya*) was given to the ruler). Conversely, the system enforced by the Almohads gave non-Muslims two options: they were allowed to leave the country or had to convert to Islam. This policy eventually led many Jews and Christians to leave Almohad territory for more tolerant Muslim lands (Bennison, 2016).

The Hafsids, a powerful group within the Almohads, trace their lineage through Umar Abu Hafs al-Hintati (d.1175), who had a close relationship with the Banu Khaldun and was a companion of Ibn Tumart. The Hafsids were initially governors of Ifriqiya (Tunisia, eastern Algeria, and western Libya) on behalf of the Almohads until their own independence in 1229. One of the many factors that led to the independence of the Hafsids was the view that subsequent Almohad rulers were no longer loyal to the original teachings of Ibn Tumart. In many respects, the Hafsids did not replace the Almohads; rather, they continued the Almohads' original teachings by staying faithful to the teachings of Ibn Tumart. In short, the Banu Hafs was the Almohad successor state. This was achieved by teaching the original doctrine of the Almohads by maintaining 'the institution of the Sheikh of the Almohads as jurist and as the most important functionary at court, and by continuing to mention the Mahdi ibn Tumart in the mosque' (Fromherz, 2011:15).

## Ibn Khaldun's Formative Years

Ibn Khaldun, or to give his full name, Abu Zayd 'Abd ar-Rahman ibn Muhammad ibn Khaldun al-Hadrami, was born in Tunis on May 27, 1332. While he is commonly known as Ibn Khaldun, his given name was 'Abd ar-Rahman and his ancestral roots are also recorded within his name: al-Hadrami or Hadramaut in Yemen. He was also known by the title, Wali-ad-din or 'Guardian of the Religion', which was attributed to him in later life. It was al-Hasan b. Muhammad, Ibn Khaldun's ancestor, who settled in Tunis under the support of the Hafsid ruler. Following al-Hasan's death, his son and Ibn Khaldun's great-grandfather, Abu Bakr Muhammad, became a prominent figure as minister of finance within the Hafsid dynasty. Ibn Khaldun's grandfather, also known as Muhammad, took early retirement from the service of the Hafsids and dedicated his life to spirituality. Muhammad would have a profound influence on Ibn Khaldun's father, also known as Muhammad, in that he pursued an intellectual life.

The lives of Ibn Khaldun's parents came to a tragic end when both of them died in the Black Death, or the Plague, which killed an estimated 75 to 200 million people and affected most of Europe and North Africa. The pandemic had a profound impact on Ibn Khaldun's worldview, given that most of his family died from it. The literature on the Plague provides an interesting insight into the diverse ways it was discussed by Muslim thinkers. Whilst some theologians explained the Plague as punishment or divine retribution, other thinkers provided more rational explanations. For example, Ibn al-Khatib and the great physician Muhammad ibn Ali ash-Shaquri (a student of Ibn al-Khatib) both made detailed notes on their empirical observations. They used clinical and rational assessments of the plague and provided advice to both the government and the public based on this (Ober and Alloush, 1982). More crucially, in the following observation Ibn Khaldun notes the overall impact of the Plague on human society by drawing links to his cyclical theory of destruction and renewal (see Chapter 4).

> The Arabs outnumbered and overpowered the Berbers of North Africa, stripped them of most of their land, and also seized the lion's share of those lands that remained in their possession. This was the situation until, in the middle of the fourteenth century, civilization in both the east and the west was visited by a destructive plague which devastated nations and caused populations to vanish. It swallowed up many of the good things of civilization and obliterated them. It over-took dynasties at the time of their senility, when they had reached the limit of their duration. It lessened their power and curtailed their influence. It weakened their authority.

Their situation approached the point of annihilation and dissolution. Civilization in the land decreased with the decrease of humanity. Great cities and monuments were laid to waste, roads and way signs were obliterated, settlements and mansions became empty, and tribes grew weak. Indeed, the entire inhabited world changed. It was as if the voice of existence had called out for oblivion, and the world had responded to its call.

(Ibn Khaldun, 1967, Vol.1: 60)

## Political Odyssey of Ibn Khaldun

Ibn Khaldun was not only a great sociologist, historian, and thinker; he was also a master political strategist. He would often pledge allegiance to one political ruler, only to abandon it and switch his loyalty. Ibn Khaldun's detailed observations of sociology, politics and history were often informed and shaped by his political career—which in turn was influenced by several political intrigues and conflicts—all of which would shape his views on the nature and function of society.

North Africa during the time of Ibn Khaldun was ruled by the Hafsid Sultan Abu Ishaq, but most of the day-to-day affairs were managed by Abu Muhammad Ibn Tafragin, the de facto ruler of Tunis. It was Ibn Tafragin who appointed Ibn Khaldun, aged only twenty in 1352, to the post of 'Master of Signature' or *Sahib al-alama*. Although the title 'Master of Signature' consisted of writing the *Basmala* or 'Praise and Thanks to God' at the top of official documents, it nevertheless gave him access to major executive functions of the state.

After serving Ibn Tafragin for two years Ibn Khaldun switches political allegiances, following a personal invitation from the Marinid Sultan, Abu Inan. This shift in loyalty is

21

due to the weak and volatile future of the Hafsids, owing to the political dominance of the Marinid sultanate in the region. It was an offer Ibn Khaldun could not refuse, especially since it meant that he would be among the Sultan's close group of advisors at the same time as dealing with wider matters of the state. This came as a welcome change for Ibn Khaldun because not only did Abu Inan have an impressive library, but he was also an erudite man who enjoyed participating in intellectual debates.

The political drama of Ibn Khaldun's life changed after he married the daughter of a Hafsid general. Whilst serving the Sultan, Ibn Khaldun was imprisoned in 1357 for conspiring against Abu Inan and supporting an anti-Marinid plot to restore Hafsid rule. Ibn Khaldun was subsequently freed from prison following the death of Abu Inan in 1358. In a remarkable twist of fate, Ibn Khaldun was now a free man, with his political position reinstated by Abu Salim, the new Marinid ruler.

It wasn't long after that Ibn Khaldun moved from the Marinid capital, Fez, to his ancestral homeland of al-Andalus in 1362. This was not a difficult move; Ibn Khaldun had supported the exiled Nasrid amir of Granada, Muhammad V, to regain his position. In return for his support Muhammad V sent Ibn Khaldun on a number of diplomatic missions, including a meeting with the King of Castile, Pedro the Cruel (d.1369) to establish a peace treaty. The King of Castile was so impressed with Ibn Khaldun that he offered him a senior post as an advisor and offered him his ancestral land in exchange for his diplomatic skills and knowledge of political life. Ibn Khaldun politely, yet firmly, declined the offer. This was primarily due to the ethical implications of advising a Christian king against his fellow Muslims, but also, Ibn Khaldun had the insight to know Pedro's days were numbered—two years later he was to die in prison. It was during his time in Granada that Ibn Khaldun developed a deep friendship with Muhammad Ibn al-Khatib (d.1374). Several academics have pointed out the profound impact of Ibn al-Khatib on Ibn Khaldun's scholarly and personal life (Fromherz, 2011). Thus, it was unsurprising that Ibn Khaldun in his *Ta'rif* considered Ibn al-Khatib as 'one of the miracles of God in the area of poetry, prose, knowledge and culture' (Irwin, 2018:32).

After falling out with Muhammad V, Ibn Khaldun is asked to leave Granada and settles back in North Africa by taking on a political role with the Hafsid *amir*, Abd Allah, in Bijaya or Bougie (currently a port city in Algeria) in 1365. Following the death of Abd Allah (in 1366), Ibn Khaldun switches loyalty for a rival Hafsid, Abu al-Abbas. As fate would have it, Abu al-Abbas was replaced by the Marinid ruler, Abu Faris al-Abd al-Aziz. The latter part of the 1360s and the early 1370s were marked by various political intrigues in Ibn Khaldun's life. By the mid-1370s, with years of political insight and experience, he settles down in a remote fortress of the Qal'at ibn Salama (currently Tiaret, Algeria) to write his magnum opus: the *Muqaddimah*.

When Ibn Khaldun retired to Qal'at ibn Salama to write his masterpiece he was a mature person, aged forty-five. Significant sections of his works were based upon memory, including quotations of various books by Ibn Arabi, Al-Masudi and others. This is a huge credit to the remarkable ability of classical scholars to memorise not only the Qur'an but also the key ancillary works. Ibn Khaldun further developed and edited his thesis once he had access to the great libraries of Egypt. His method of writing the *Muqaddimah* has been criticised by several writers due to various errors, misquotations and incorrect referencing of sources (see Rosenthal, 1958:lxix–lxxi). Despite this, in true testament to his erudition, Ibn Khaldun managed to complete the *Muqaddimah* in less than five months (Enan 1993:52), although he would continue to revise the work until its publication. Once this monumental work was complete, Ibn Khaldun wrote the following words of poetry in recognition of the patronage and support given by Sultan Abu al-Abbas. It began with the following:

> Here in the histories of time and people are lessons the morals of which are followed by the just. I summarised all the books of the ancients. And recorded what they omitted. I smoothed the methods of expression as if they submitted to my will. I dedicate it, a glory, to your realm, which shines, and is the object of pride. I swear that I did not exaggerate what is hateful to me.
>
> (Cited in Enan 1993:52)

## Ibn Khaldun in Cairo

Ibn Khaldun settles his differences with the Hafsid ruler and under the pretext of making Hajj leaves and settles in Cairo, Egypt, in 1382. Cairo was the capital of the Mamluk Sultanate, which controlled most of Egypt, the Levant, and the Hijaz from 1250 until 1517. It is clear from his own writing that Ibn Khaldun was completely taken aback by the grandeur and sophistication of the city; this is one of many reasons why he chose to remain in Cairo until his death in 1406. For Ibn Khaldun, Cairo was seen as the 'city of the world', 'garden of the universe' and the 'assemblage of multitudes of mankind'. Cairo in the latter part of the fourteenth century was more enlightened and cosmopolitan than other cities, such as Fez, Granada and Tunis. Ibn Khaldun was so impressed by Cairo, he made the following observation in his autobiography:

> [Cairo] Capital of the world, garden of the universe, forum for the gatherings of people ... palaces of Islam, throne of power, a city, a city embellished with palaces and mansions, ornamented with colleges and schools, its scholars are like shining stars. The city lay across the Nile, river of paradise, receptacle of heavenly water... One could not stop speaking of this city, of its high degree of civilisation, of its prosperity.
> (Cited in Fromherz, 2011:97)

As soon as Ibn Khaldun arrived in Cairo, his reputation as a historian and a leading figure on the North-African political stage attracted considerable attention from students. In the early days Ibn Khaldun started to teach Islamic jurisprudence and aspects of his *Muqaddimah* at the famous Al-Azhar University. Al-Azhar is one of the oldest universities in the world, established by the Fatimid dynasty in 970 and continues to teach and grant degrees to this day. Ibn Khaldun's lectures at the university had a profound impact on the "affairs of the state" and the segments of the *Muqaddimah* had a lasting impact on the student population in Cairo (Dale, 2015:143).

It wasn't long until the Mamluk Sultan, Al-Malik al-Zahir Barquq (1399), developed an admiration for and strong friendship with Ibn Khaldun, and as a result appointed him

25

to teach Maliki-Islamic jurisprudence at the famous Qamhiya madrasa. In addition to his teaching and professorial role at the Qamhiya, Ibn Khaldun was also appointed as the chief Maliki judge of Egypt. When this prestigious role was offered to him by Sultan Barquq, he initially refused to take it on. It was only after the insistence of the Sultan that he gladly accepted the honour accorded to him by his protector and patron (Fischel, 1967).

As a judge Ibn Khaldun represented the Maliki School of Islamic jurisprudence, which was of a lower rank than the dominant Shafi'i school. The Mamluks had a judicial system which represented all four schools of thought. Nevertheless, it is clear from Ibn Khaldun's autobiography that he was adamant 'to administer God's law with utmost justice'. This meant that he had to conduct his affairs as 'fairly and in an exemplary manner ... without any concern for the [accused] status or power in society ... [by focusing] on finding the truth only by attending to the evidence' (Kosei, 2002:112). Ibn Khaldun was quick to identify corruption amongst people in authority, who were 'dishonest or lacking in morals' due to passing judgments on unethical practice, such as administering justice based upon an individual's status in society. In doing so, Ibn Khaldun was able to expose the moral decay which 'ran deep among the official witnesses, and within such a deceit-ridden corrupt administration, the decay spread from one person to the next' (ibid.).

Some of the above 'decay and corruption' observed by Ibn Khaldun revolved around usurpation of *waqf* property or charitable endowments, such as educational, religious, or similar charitable centres by the state. Typically, the process would include *waqf* properties targeted by people in power, who would then use corrupt judges to invalidate or give judgments so that these properties could be confiscated by the state (Kosei, 2002:115). Ibn Khaldun notes how some of these judges were not only corrupt, but also lacked any true and serious Islamic learning.

> Still, I set about reforming this [habit] by arresting the muftis who were quacks or who lacked learning, and I punished them firmly. Among them, however, was a number of Maghribis who gathered together and dazzled people by rattling off jargon, although they themselves had neither studied under a great master (shaykh) nor versed themselves in specialist texts. They trifled with people's feelings, turning the court into a place where prominent people were slandered and those deserving of respect were insulted. They hated me because of the punishments I meted out, so they joined forces with the inhabitants of those monasteries promoting the same kind of belief as theirs. The appearance of piety that this allegiance lent them brought them a level of prestige, which they then abused in impious ways. Good people would inevitably choose them as arbitrators, at which they would gabble their chants as if with the voice of Satan, then claim that all was solved. Being unmoved by religion, their ignorance leads them to expose the laws of God to danger.
>
> (Ibn Khaldun, autobiography cited in Kosei, 2002:112)

In light of the above observation, it can be argued that backlash against Ibn Khaldun was inevitable, especially since many people were impacted financially by his exposure of corruption. The response came in the guise of character assassination, with some scholars arguing that Ibn Khaldun was ignorant of Islamic law and jurisprudence. A number of people also started to spread false rumours and attempt to defile his name by inventing lies about him; all of this was done to ensure that Ibn Khaldun passed favourable judgments in support of the dignitaries. Ibn Khaldun mentions in his autobiography how despite the defamation campaign, he 'rebuffed temptations toward injustice, and firmly refused to be influenced by prestige or riches, even when this resulted in my name being slandered' (ibid). Whilst Ibn Khaldun mentions that the Sultan came to hear about the rumours and continued to support him, this was not to last, and he was eventually removed from the prestigious post of Maliki judge in 1385. Ibn Khaldun writes the following observation on this matter:

> I broke up their malevolent circle and chastised their clients, in accordance with the laws of God. Their cronies in the monasteries became powerless, since people stopped going there, so their well [their source of funds] dried up. Having thus lost their clientele these foolish people flew into a rage. They tried to defile my honour, inventing and spreading twisted, false rumours about me. Even the sultan came to hear rumours of my wrongs. The sultan, however, did not listen to them; the consequences of what I had put in motion were in the hands of God. Thus, I paid no heed to the ignorant and walked the path of courage and rigour. I took equality and righteousness as my guides, rebuffed temptations toward injustice, and firmly refused to be influenced by prestige or riches, even when this resulted in my name being slandered. Such a course of action was not adopted by my colleagues: they disavowed my counsel and advised me to follow their example in appeasing the government

officials and showing consideration toward those with influence. In other words, in clear cut cases I should pass judgments favourable to the dignitaries, and when there were difficulties I should reject the case, since when there were other judges [within the same circle of jurisdiction] there was no obligation for one judge to pass judgment.

(Ibid.).

Despite the removal of Ibn Khaldun as Maliki judge, he was able to continue his teaching and professorial duties at the Qamhiya *madrasah*. In 1388, after his return from Hajj he was given two additional appointments as a teacher of hadith at Salghatmish *madrasah* and the head of the Sufi Khanqah, named after Mamluk Sultan Baibars (d.1277). This glory was short-lived, especially when Sultan Barquq, who had supported Ibn Khaldun with his patronage, was briefly imprisoned (1389) after an attempted *coup d'état*. Sultan Barquq was able to reign again from 1390 until his death in 1399. In 1399 Ibn Khaldun was also reinstated as Maliki judge, a position he would continue to regain and lose amid various controversies until his death in 1406 (Enan 1993; Alatas 2013). In total, Ibn Khaldun was appointed six times (Alatas, 2012).

The last seven years of Ibn Khaldun's life were also highly eventful. Following the death of Sultan Barquq, the Mamluk dynasty was passed to his son Sultan an-Nasir Farjaj (d.1411). The death of Sultan Barquq also gave Tamerlane or Timur (d.1405) the opportunity to take over Cairo. Timur was the founder of the Timurid Empire and the successor to Genghis Khan; he is ranked amongst other renowned world conquerors such as Alexander the Great. Timur was a complex individual: 'the character of Timur has been differently appraised by those who are dazzled by his military achievements on the one hand and those who are disgusted by his cruelty and utter disregard of human life on the other' (Browne, cited in Marozzi, 2004:3). In fact, some of the strongest vocal critics of Timur, such as the fifteenth-century Syrian chronicler Ahmed ibn Arabshah, described one of the aftermaths of Timur's raids: 'wild beast seemed collected and scattered over the earth... when his army flowed hither and thither... the earth seemed shaken by violent movement' (Marozzi, 2004:3). Despite such strong views, Arabshah also recognised Timur's admiration for scholars and saints, and respect for science and learning. These traits would work in Ibn Khaldun's favour during the infamous meetings in Damascus:

> Timur loved learned men and admitted to his inner reception nobles of the family of Mohammed: he gave the highest honour to the learned and doctors and preferred them to all others and received each of them according to his rank and granted them honour and respect; he used towards them familiarity and an abatement of his majesty; in his arguments with them he mingled moderation with splendour, clemency with rigour and covered his severity with kindness.
>
> (Arabshah, cited in Marozzi 2004:88)

Timur left a legacy of destruction by invading parts of Syria, especially through his capture of the great city of Aleppo. Concerned by the death, destruction and bloodshed, which became the signature marks of Mongol invasion, al-Fajaj began to advance his troops with a view to stop the Mongols. Al-Fajaj was accompanied by several scholars, Sufis and jurists; among them was Ibn Khaldun, as it was acceptable practice under the Mamluks to entrust scholars and judges on military or diplomatic missions (Fischel, 1967). Upon arrival at Damascus, al-Fajaj had to retreat due to rumours of a political plot against him in Cairo, leaving Ibn Khaldun and others behind. The inhabitants of Damascus were puzzled when they realised that they were left without the Sultan or any of his amirs. It was within this context of confusion 'that the leaders of Damascus decided, after consulting Ibn Khaldun... to accept Tamerlane's offer of an armistice' (Fischel, 1967:44). It wasn't long until the capture and surrender of Damascus was finally sealed by Timur, with Ibn Khaldun and others trapped inside the city wall. Ibn Khaldun was able to use his political and diplomatic skills to negotiate an audience with Timur with the view of arranging a safe passage back to Cairo. Ibn Khaldun's reputation as a writer and statesman enabled him to have a series of meetings with the Mongol ruler from 10 January 1401, until 25 [or 27] February 1401, the most likely date of his departure from Damascus.

The frequency of Ibn Khaldun's meetings with the great conqueror is a testimony and confirmation of Ibn Khaldun's stature as a historian and statesman. According to Ibn Khaldun's own accounts, he was in attendance with Timur and his council for thirty-five days (or occasions). It is claimed that Timur was impressed by Ibn Khaldun's critical grasp of history and his detailed knowledge of North Africa. The key topics that were discussed by Ibn Khaldun and Timur were documented by the former, for posterity, and captured below:

1. On the Maghrib and Ibn Khaldun's land of origin.
2. On heroes in history.
3. On predictions of things to come.

4. On the Abbasid caliphate.
5. On amnesty and security: 'Concerning Myself and some Companions of mine'.
6. On Ibn Khaldun's intention to stay with Tamerlane.

(Cited in, Fischel, 1967:49)

The infamous meeting between the scholar and the conqueror resulted in a request from Timur for Ibn Khaldun to write an account of North African history. Ibn Khaldun was able to write twelve treatises on North Africa, which were presented to Timur, who ordered them to be translated into native Mongolian language. The exact content of these treatises is unknown; however, it is assumed that they would have been based upon observations contained in *Kitab al-Ibar* (Enan, 1933). Two months later, Ibn Khaldun did manage to secure a safe passage from Timur for himself and other scholars and bureaucrats in February or March 1401. Also, as history informs us, the Mamluks managed to defeat the Timurid Empire. After returning to Cairo, Ibn Khaldun was re-appointed as Maliki judge. Ibn Khaldun spent most of his later life completing his autobiography together with teaching and fulfilling his role as a judge. Having spent twenty-three years in Egypt, only leaving for three brief sojourns, Ibn Khaldun passed away on 26 Ramadan 1406, following a long and intriguing career as a political advisor, scholar, judge and Sufi. He is buried in the Sufi cemetery, Cairo.

# Table 1

## *Ibn Khaldun: A Timeline*

| Date | Summary |
|------|---------|
| 711 | Tariq ibn Ziyad captures South of Spain from the Visigoths. Muslims would rule Spain until 1492. The region is called al-Andalus. |
| Early eighth century | The Khaldun family move to al-Andalus and settle in the city of Seville. |
| Late ninth century | An independent principality of Seville is declared following a revolt against the Umayyad *amir* by Kurayb Ibn Khaldun, a distant ancestor of Ibn Khaldun. |
| Circa. 1039–1147 | The Almoravid or Murabitun dynasty begins. It expands from north-western Mauritania to Morocco, Algeria and Southern Spain. |
| 1147–1229 | The Almohads or al-Muwahidun or 'those who profess the *tawhid*,' succeed in overthrowing the Almoravids. During their peak they would control all of North Africa and Southern Spain. |

| Date | Summary |
|------|---------|
| 1229–1574 | The Hafsids, a powerful group of governors, emerge within the Almohad dynasty. They declare independence from the Almohads and argue that the Almohads are not loyal to the teachings of the Almohad founder Ibn Tumart. Since the 1230s the Hafsids have had strong political ties with the Khaldun family. They would rule from Tunis as their capital. |
| 1244–1465 | The Marinid sultanate is established. They would rule from Morocco and have intermittent control over the Hafsids. |
| 1248 | The Reconquista of Muslim Spain by the Christian army takes a critical turning point with the capture of Seville by King Ferdinand III of Castile. Christian armies have already taken Toledo in 1085. Prior to the capture of Seville, the Khaldun family leave for North Africa (Hafsid rule). |
| 1332 | Ibn Khaldun is born in Tunis. |
| 1348–49 | Ibn Khaldun's parents die in the Plague. |
| 1352 | Ibn Khaldun, at the age of 22, is appointed by Ibn Tafragin (de-facto leader of the Hafsid dynasty) as 'Master of Signature'. |

| Date | Summary |
|------|---------|
| 1354 | Ibn Khaldun accepts the invitation from the Marinid sultan, Abu Inan. Ibn Khaldun moves to Fez. |
| 1354 | Ibn Khaldun marries the daughter of a Hafsid general. |
| 1357 | After conspiring against Abu Inan, Ibn Khaldun is sent to prison for supporting an anti-Marinid plot to restore Hafsid rule. |
| 1358 | Abu Inan dies. Ibn Khaldun is freed and his political position reinstated by the new Marinid ruler, Abu Salim. |
| 1362 | Ibn Khaldun supports the exiled (Fez) Nasrid *amir* of Granada, Muhammad V, to regain his position there. In the same year Ibn Khaldun arrives in Granada. He develops a close relationship with Ibn al-Khatib. |
| 1364 | As part of his diplomatic role Ibn Khaldun is sent to meet Pedro the Cruel in Seville. |
| 1365 | After falling out with Muhammad V, Ibn Khaldun leaves Granada and takes on a senior position under the Hafsid ruler Abd Allah. A year later Abd Allah dies. He gives allegiance to Abdul Abas, a rival Hafsid ruler. |
| 1365–1377 | North Africa is marked by political turmoil. |

| Date | Summary |
|------|---------|
| 1377 | Ibn Khaldun, at the age of 45, settles down to write his *Muqaddimah* in a remote part of Algeria. |
| 1378–1382 | Ibn Khaldun settles his differences with the Hafsid ruler and under the pretext of making Hajj, leaves and settles in Cairo, Egypt. |
| 1382 | At the age of 50, Ibn Khaldun settles in Cairo. He keeps himself busy with teaching, writing and working as a Maliki judge. |
| 1401 | Ibn Khaldun meets Tamerlane. |
| 1406 | At the age of 74, Ibn Khaldun passes away after spending 24 years in Cairo. |

# Chapter 2

## *Knowledge, Education and Pedagogy*

**M**uslim societies hold a unique position compared with other religious communities, in that the first revelation of the Qur'an commands the believers to 'read'. The final revelation to mankind encourages the believers to ponder and reflect upon the signs of Allah through a variety of rich metaphors drawing upon nature, cosmology and society. Indeed, the Qur'an (39:9) commands, 'Say, "How can those who know be equal to those who do not know?" Only those who have understanding will take heed.' Hadith literature also reinforces the above command by reminding the believers that 'seeking knowledge is obligatory for every Muslim'. Classical Muslim scholars spent considerable amount of ink trying to understand the above passages dealing with knowledge in Islam. Is the pursuit of knowledge restricted to religion? Or does it include knowledge gained through reason, such as science, history, medicine and philosophy? Ibn Khaldun's education was shaped by religious and philosophical sciences; both branches of knowledge influenced his commitment to revelation and reason. It is clear from a measured reading of the *Muqaddimah* that Ibn Khaldun did not see any difficulty in 'simultaneously affirming the truth of Muhammad's (saw) prophetic message and, while vigorously asserting the validity of reason when it came to examining the external world, including the arena of society and politics' (Dale 2015:74).

Ibn Khaldun appreciated the significance of education and learning, especially given the central role it plays in sustaining civilisation and civilised life. The role of education and the pursuit of knowledge was also a mainstay of Islam, as highlighted in the classical study titled *Knowledge Triumphant: The Concept of Knowledge in Medieval Islam* by Francis Rosenthal (1970). Rosenthal noted the problematic nature of translating *ilm* as "knowledge" because it fails to capture the factual and emotional expression embodied within the concept of *ilm* (Rosenthal, 1970:2), especially given that it is a key concept that has dominated Islam and given Muslim civilisation its distinctive shape and complexion. In fact, there is no other concept that has been as critical in determining the direction of Muslim civilisation in all its aspects than the pursuit and dissemination of *ilm*. Indeed, various scholars were bold enough to make the claim that there are very few ideas within Islam that carry depth of meaning and wide range of use than *ilm*, which led many of them to conclude that '*ilm* is Islam'. This is because there is 'no branch of Muslim intellectual life, of Muslim religious and political life, and of the daily life of the average Muslim that remained untouched by the all-pervasive attitude toward "knowledge" as something of supreme value for Muslim being' (ibid.).

A detailed survey of the role of *ilm* within classical Muslim civilisation demonstrates how the concept was a relational category, especially with other concepts such as *hikmah* (wisdom), *adl* (justice) and *haqq* (truth). For example, the *Kitab al-Huquq* of *al-Hikam* by Imam at-Tirmidhi (d.892) states 'God brought forth knowledge (*ilm*) in the beginning. From knowledge he brought forth wisdom (*hikmah*). From wisdom He brought forth justice (*adl*) and truth (*haqq*)' (Cited in Rosenthal, 1970:38). The emphasis placed upon the pursuit of knowledge during the 'golden period' of classical Islam no doubt made 'Muslim civilisation one of great scholarly and scientific productivity, and through it, Muslim civilisation made its most lasting contribution to mankind' (Rosenthal 1970:3). By drawing upon Ibn Khaldun's writing on knowledge and education, this chapter provides the centrality of knowledge as a broad and inclusive category in determining, nurturing, and sustaining civilisations. In doing so, we can see how much can be achieved by the fusion of intellectual and spiritual values through the pursuit and dissemination of knowledge. Furthermore, this chapter provides an outline of Ibn Khaldun's personal education, which was largely shaped by the need to continue the family tradition of the scholar-official.

## Ibn Khaldun: Education and Upbringing

Ibn Khaldun's main teacher and mentor during his early years was his father, Muhammad Abu Bakr, who played a crucial role in shaping his views on education and learning. More critically, it was his father, who sadly died when Ibn Khaldun was 16 years old, who instilled in him a love and appreciation for the study of the Qur'an and Sufism (see Chapter 3). In some respects, Ibn Khaldun's education was typical for most educated people of his time, in that he had memorised the Qur'an at an early age, studied *hadith*, excelled in Maliki jurisprudence and mastered poetry, mathematics, medicine, history, literature and philosophy. Like most families of the time, the Bani Khaldun held the pursuit of learning in high esteem, thus the family frequently welcomed scholars, jurists and poets into their home. The young and astute Ibn Khaldun greatly benefitted from this close interaction and proximity to scholars, which as we will see, would have a profound impact on his later life. From a young age he was also interested in the practical affairs of government. As a result, he embarked on an apprenticeship, which included specialized training in the art of writing official court correspondence and of managing routine administrative and bureaucratic matters. This practical skill would prove very useful during his time as a political advisor.

Perhaps what was unconventional for Ibn Khaldun was that he did not study in any prestigious *madrasah*s or Islamic seminaries; rather, he continued his one-to-one studies with various notable teachers in a range of disciplines. Given the nature of his education, Ibn Khaldun is often recognised through his teachers and not institutional affiliations. One of the main teachers who had a profound impact on him was the philosopher and mathematician Al-Abili of Tlemcen (note the diverse spellings of his name). Whilst Al-Abili is not well-known outside the learned communities, especially given that none of his works have survived, it appears that he taught a generation of students over the course of his life. Al-Abili had an encyclopaedic grasp of a range of disciplines, including matters of religion, philosophy, medicine and reason. As a rationalist himself, Al-Abili authored many commentaries on the rational thinkers such as Ibn Rushd, Ibn Sina, Al-Farabi and Al-Razi. A further biographical account of Al-Abili provided by Ibn Khaldun provides a glimpse into the world of a polymath.

> Back in the West, Al-Abilyy continued to study philosophy and tried to avoid being inducted into government service as chief treasurer, where his knowledge of mathematics could be put to use. He fled to Fez, hiding in the house of the Jewish mathematician Khallûf al-Maghili, where he continued to study mathematics. Later he went to Marrâkush to study mysticism, mathematics, and philosophy, with the 'master of the West' Abû al-'Abbâs Ahmad Ibn al-Bannâ (d. 1321). Soon, he became the most celebrated teacher and 'the most proficient of his contemporaries in the philosophic sciences'. Abilyy was among the scholars accompanying the Marinid ruler Abû al-Hasan to Tunis in 1347/748. There he met Ibn Khaldun's father and lodged in his household. Through his father, Ibn Khaldun, though still a young man of sixteen, was able to attend Abilyy's circle.
>
> (Mehdi, 1957:35)

One of the advantages of living in a politically influential and privileged family is that Ibn Khaldun's teacher and mentor stayed in the Khaldun household. As a result, Ibn Khaldun's learning was not restricted to fixed hours of teaching determined by a structure. Rather, flexible learning allowed Ibn Khaldun to develop a detailed grasp of religion and philosophy. The impact of rationalism on Ibn Khaldun through Al-Abili is clearly demonstrated through his early work, aged only 19:

> A manuscript discovered in the Escorial library in early 1950s turned out to be a long essay written by the young Ibn Khaldun when he was a student of Al-Ibili. Something of an exam paper or final project for his master, Al-Ibili, the *Lubab al-Muhassal fi usul al-din* testified to Ibn Khaldun's early grasp of philosophical and theological material of the *Takhlis al-Muhassal*, a standard work on *kalam*, or Islamic theology, by the important exegete Umar ibn al-Khatib al Razi (d.1209). He also analysed the works of its contemporary Nasir al-Din al-Tusi (1274).
>
> (Fromherz 2011:45)

Ibn Khaldun's education in many ways went against the normative model of learning for his time, whereby students attended the prestigious centres of learning throughout North Africa, although he would end up teaching in many of these institutions in later life. There was no shortage of prestigious institutions in North Africa. For example, there was the famous Ben Youssef Madrasa in Morocco, named after the Almoravid Sultan Ali ibn Youssef, who ruled from 1106 until 1142, and the University of al-Qarawiyyin, Fez, Morocco. Al-Qarawiyyin is one of the oldest continuously operating higher education institutes in the world, established in 859 by a Muslim woman, Fatima al-Fihri. After building the famous Al-Qarawiyyin Mosque Fatima al-Fihri built the University of Al-Qarawiyyin as an extension to the original mosque—both institutions were funded using inheritance received from her father, and she personally oversaw both of the projects herself. The university also has one of the oldest libraries in the world; it is often said that Ibn Khaldun donated one of his copies of the *Kitab al-Ibar* to it.

## On Weak Teachers

Ibn Khaldun's views on *madrasah*s were highly influenced by his teacher and mentor Al-Abili. Al-Abili's critique of formal education was due to the politicisation of the schooling system with the encroaching influence of rulers. 'True science,' he argued, 'should be free from political influence.' Failure to achieve this would cause significant damage to the child and wider society. Furthermore, political influence in the guise of material benefits may also lead to the corrupting influence of teachers. This is clearly recorded by the historian al-Maqqari (d.1632):

> [according to al-Abili] students are attracted by the scholarship and material benefits offered there and go to the teachers designated by the government to govern and teach in these madrasas, or to teachers who have agreed to subject themselves to the authorities. This separates the students from [those other] teachers who represent true science and who have not been appointed to the madrasas, for if they had been appointed they would have refused and had they accepted it would not be to fulfil the role demanded of the others.
>
> (Cited in herz, 2011:46)

43

For Ibn Khaldun, true knowledge is not embedded within a given institutional structure, especially given that these institutions often serve the cultural or political interests of the rulers. The politicisation of education is evident throughout history; it was common for rulers to apply pressure on educational institutions in order to promote a certain theological position, which would serve the interests of that ruler. It could be argued that Ibn Khaldun was ahead of his time in his political critiques of education. The idea that educational institutions serve the interests of the 'state' or the political masters of the day as opposed to 'educating' the future generations of children with knowledge, skills and ethics is a rather modern idea within the sociology of education (Mayo and Miah, 2021).

Ibn Khaldun promoted an independent approach to education whilst manifesting a precarious relationship with educational institutions. He was sceptical of the idea that fixed forms of learning were superior to organic models. Ibn Khaldun was also deeply critical of the institutionalisation of teaching and the impact this had on teachers. He considers these teachers as 'rootless' due to not serving the interests and the true spirit of religious duty and obligation, but political motives. On a more critical note, he considers the teachers to be 'misled by their desires', often taking up positions that they are not interested in nor capable of fulfilling. This is clear from the following observation:

> At the present time, teaching is a craft and serves to make a living. It is a far cry from the pride of group feeling. Teachers are weak, indigent and rootless. Many weak professional

men and artisans who work for a living aspire to positions for which they are not fit but which they believe to be within their reach. They are misled by their desires, a rope which often slips from their hands and precipitates them into the abyss of ruinous perdition. They do not realise that what they desire is impossible for men like them to attain. And they do not know that at the beginning of Islam and during the (Umayyad and Abbasid) dynasties, teaching was something different.

(Ibn Khaldun, 1958, Vol.1: 58–59)

Ibn Khaldun contrasts the educational system and the teachers of his time with the formative years of Islam, especially the Prophetic model of education with its emphasis on 'transmission of traditions' in teaching. In doing so, he makes a significant point on pedagogy and how education should be about transmission of religious traditions and not professional instruction. This is further exemplified by the following:

Scholarship, in general, was not a craft in that period. Scholarship was transmitting statements that people had heard the Lawgiver (Muhammad saw) make. It was teaching religious matters that were not known, by way of oral transmission. Persons of noble descent and people who shared in the group feeling of (the ruling dynasty) and who directed the affairs of Islam were the ones who taught the Book of God and Sunnah of the Prophet, (and they did so) as one transmits tradition, not as one gives professional instruction. (The Qur'an) was their scripture, revealed to the Prophet in their midst. It constituted their guidance, and Islam was their religion, and for it they fought and died. It distinguished them from other nations and ennobled them. They wished to teach it and make it understandable to the

Muslims. They were not deterred by censure coming from pride, nor were they restrained by criticism coming from arrogance. This is attested by the fact that the Prophet sent the most important of men around him with his embassies to the Arabs, in order to teach them the norms of Islam and the religious law he brought. He sent his ten companions and others after them on this mission.

(Ibn Khaldun, 1958, Vol.1: 59)

The above views articulated by Ibn Khaldun in his *Muqaddimah* may have been motivated by the misuse of the educational system in his time. A number of academics have also pointed out that his concerns may have been motivated in part by the creeping influence of the great Hanbali scholar, Ibn Taymiyya (d.1328) on the Marinid Sultanate (Hoover, 2020). Ibn Khaldun's criticism of the madrasa system may have also been due to his firm position on Sufism; a practice which he felt was undermined and increasingly challenged by some within the Merinid Sultanate, under the influence of Hanbalite critique of Sufism. The relationship between the ruler, education and Sufism is further articulated below:

> Ibn Khaldun's strong criticism of the Maliki madrasas was his defence of the Islamic mysticism, or Sufism, practised by his father, and although less overtly by himself... the purpose of the Marinid madrasa was the promotion of a certain common 'epistemology based upon legal reason'. The Marinid emphasis on jurisprudential education was 'a revival of juridical arguments against Sufism'.
>
> (Fromherz, 2011:47)

## Khaldunian Classification of Knowledge

In classical Muslim civilisation, the concept of knowledge was central to the fabric of society. Indeed, the Qur'an repeatedly encourages believers to think, reflect and ponder. Following the advice of the Prophet Muhammad (saw) to 'seek knowledge, even if you have to travel to China', the concept of *rihla*, or travel in pursuit of education and learning became an established feature of most scholarly endeavour. Thus, it is not surprising that classification of knowledge as an ethical commitment became an established genre of study (Sardar, 2020).

In light of the religious duty to seek *ilm*, Muslim societies were actively involved with knowledge production, classification, and dissemination, with many scholars and philosophers throughout the centuries developing their own epistemological approaches. Many early Muslim thinkers ranging from al-Farabi, Ibn Rushd, Ibn Tufail and al-Ghazali dedicated their lives to the pursuit of knowledge. It is not surprising that Muslim thinkers came up with over 500 definitions of knowledge, covering a wide range of areas, including divine knowledge, scientific knowledge, and spiritual knowledge (Rosenthal 1970:52–69). More crucially, classical Muslim scholarship identified three distinct approaches to knowledge: Knowledge as Islam, Knowledge as Light and Knowledge as Thought (Rosenthal, 1970). The religious scholars maintained that knowledge is Islam, especially knowledge which is revealed through the sacred text and the guidance embodied within the Prophet Muhammad's (saw) conduct and actions. They argued how 'right from the start the student of Qur'an finds himself confronted with the thought presented forcefully and inescapably that all human knowledge that has any real value and truly deserves to be called "knowledge" is religious knowledge' (Rosenthal 1970:30). The Sufis and those who pursue a mystical path to Islam took the more esoteric view of knowledge as light. 'Light' is a metaphorical term which holds symbolic value within Sufism and is often contrasted with 'darkness' and 'ignorance'. For Sufis, true knowledge comes through revelation, discovery (often through the aid of a spiritual master) and inspiration. Perhaps the importance of knowledge as light is best captured by Mawlana Rumi (d.1273) in his *Masnavi* (Mojeddedi, 2014). Rumi sees the importance of Arabic grammar, Islamic theology and related textual knowledge; however, without knowledge of the spiritual path a person is incomplete. This is captured eloquently by the following reminder:

> He knows countless chapters of the sciences
> But that wrongdoer does not know his soul
> He knows the properties of every essence
> But can he tell his own essence from an ass?
> 'I know what is licit, what's illicit'
> But what about yourself? You cannot say
> If you're licit or illiterate...
> You know religion's grounds and rules, and yet
> Look to your own roots, are they sound or not?
> Rumi (2008) 3:2648–56

Several academics have questioned the view that 'truth' can be achieved via the greatness of Sufi masters. True knowledge, they argue, can only be found within revealed scriptures, available to all believers and not the select few (al-Jawziyya, 2016).

Finally, the philosophers and some Muslim theologians viewed 'knowledge as thought' as incorporating something much broader and complex, including the epistemological worldviews of the Greek and Hellenistic philosophers. For example, for the Muslim philosopher al-Farabi writing in the tenth century, knowledge is structured upon the hierarchical ordering of the sciences. Students were encouraged to concentrate their studies based upon the methodological, ontological and ethical merits of knowledge. The methodological merits were drawn from hierarchical ordering of proofs, arguments and the modes of knowing things; the ontological was based upon the ranking of the universe and the ethical merits were based upon prioritisation of human needs and goals (Bakar 1998:263).

Some scholars attempted to merge the above three classifications of knowledge. In the twelfth century, the Muslim theologian al-Ghazali viewed the relationship between knowledge and discipline through religious sciences and the intellectual sciences. Religious sciences are 'those which have been acquired from the prophets and are not arrived at by reason, like arithmetic, or by experimentation, like medicine, or by hearing, like language' (al-Ghazali cited in Bakar 1998:205). The intellectual sciences include disciplines that are attained through the human rational faculties. For al-Ghazali, the religious and the intellectual sciences should be seen to complement and not contradict each other—the distinction between the two is determined by the sources of each knowledge. The intellectual sciences are based upon reason and as a result are subservient to religious sciences, since the latter are based upon revelation (ibid.).

Ibn Khaldun provides his own classification of knowledge based upon three key sciences which existed in Muslim civilisation during his time, namely: Traditional, Intellectual and the Magical sciences. The Traditional Sciences according to Ibn Khaldun are based upon knowledge grounded in revelation. The crucial element of the Traditional Sciences is that the basic character remains unchanged, thus limiting the role of the intellect. This is based on the argument that 'information based upon the authority of the given religious law. There is no place for the intellect in them, save that the intellect may be used in connection with them to relate problems of detail with basic principles' (Ibn Khaldun, 1958: 436). The Traditional Sciences consist of different types of sciences associated with the Qur'an and Sunnah such as auxiliary disciplines, including Arabic language (see below). Ibn Khaldun further notes how the expansion of Islam within non-Arabic speaking lands opened up the possibility of corruption of the Arabic language. It is the significance of the Qur'an and the Sunnah which preserve Islam and in turn help preserve the Arabic language (Ibn Khaldun, 1958, Vol.1: 307).

### Traditional Sciences (Alatas, 2013:83)

#### Sciences of the Qur'an
- Interpretation
- Recitation

#### Sciences of the Arabic Language
- Lexicography
- Grammar
- Syntax and Style

– Literature

**Sciences of Prophetic Tradition**
– Ulum al-Hadith

**Jurisprudence**
– Usul al-fiqh

**Speculative Theology**
– Ilm al-Kalam

**Sufism**

**Sciences of Dream**

The second branch of knowledge according to Ibn Khaldun's classification are the Intellectual Sciences, covering a wide range of disciplines, including both the natural and the social sciences. These are important because they allow people to become 'acquainted through the very nature of one's ability to think and to whose objects, problems, arguments, and methods of instruction he is guided by his human perception' (Ibn Khaldun, 1958: Vol.2: 436). These sciences were cultivated by two pre-Islamic civilisations, namely the Persian and Greek. The bulk of this knowledge was translated into Arabic through major centres in Baghdad, such as the House of Wisdom or *Bayt al-Hikma* during the reign of the Abbasid caliphs Harun al-Rashid and Al-Ma'mun in the late eighth century. The House of Wisdom became a leading centre in translating all ancient wisdoms, from mathematics and astronomy to philosophy and medicine. Ibn Khaldun (1958) notes how Muslim scientists not only studied the Greek scientists but a number of them, such as Ibn Sina and Ibn Rushd, became leading experts in their respective fields. In doing so they were able to find and correct contradictions in the works of the First Teacher (Aristotle) and as a result were able to surpass their Greek predecessors in the intellectual sciences. More crucially, he notes how 'the intellectual sciences and their representatives succeeded to some degree in penetrating Islam. This seduced many people who were eager to study those sciences and accept the opinions expressed in them' (Ibn Khaldun, 1958).

### Intellectual Sciences (Ibn Khaldun, 1958, Volume 3: 111–156)

**Physics**
- Celestial and Elementary bodies
- Zoology
- Botany
- Chemistry
- Minerals
- Psychology
- Medicine
- Agriculture
- Seismology

**Science of Logic**

**Metaphysics**

**Mathematical Sciences**
- Geometry
- Music
- Arithmetic
- Astronomy
- Atmospheric sciences

Finally, the third system of knowledge includes the occult sciences, which are forbidden under Islamic law. The sciences of magic and sorcery have their origins in non-Islamic societies, and were regularly practised by the Copts, the Babylonians and the Chaldeans. Despite their origins, the practice of magic and sorcery became widespread throughout Muslim societies (Ahmed, 2003:87). Ibn Khaldun stresses how these sciences are forbidden not only by Islam but also by various other religions, because 'they are harmful and require (their practitioners) to direct themselves to (beings) other than God, such as stars and other things. Therefore, books dealing with them are almost non-existent among the people' (Ibn Khaldun, 1958, Vol.3: 156).

## Science of Magic and Sorcery (Ibn Khaldun, 1958, Volume 3: 156–246)

**Sorcery**                          **Talisman**
– Letter magic or *simiya*
– Alchemy

## Educational Pedagogy within Classical Islam

Pedagogy, or the method and practice of teaching, is often associated with contemporary educational theory. In fact, the study of how to teach has now become an academic discipline in itself, with a vast number of journals and books devoted to the topic. Countless studies have demonstrated the critical importance of actions, judgments and strategies adopted by the given teacher in determining the educational outcome of the student. Given the importance of education, it is unsurprising to see early Muslim scholars devote considerable amount of attention to the study of educational pedagogy; some of these names include al-Farabi (d.872), Ibn Sina (d.1037), al-Jahiz (d.869) and al-Ghazali (d.1111).

For classical Muslim thinkers, educational aims and objectives revolve around the following discussions. First, education was a key instrument in attaining God-consciousness, thus the lifelong pursuit of learning was associated with good character and piety. Several Muslim thinkers, including Ibn Rushd (d.1198), considered the importance of character, piety, and God-consciousness as crucial educational objectives. Moreover, al-Farabi (d.872) and more significantly Ibn Tufail (d.1185), through his philosophical novel *Hayy ibn Yaqdhan*, highlighted the importance of critical thinking within education.

Second, Muslim thinkers, including Ibn Khaldun, stressed the importance of correct ethical conduct of children and adults. They argue that education should not simply be measured by the capacity for memorisation; an educated person is not an embodiment of 'data' but rather determined by the refinement of character. Thus, the memorisation of the Qur'an and related textual sciences should not be seen as an end in itself, but a means of achieving good character. Indeed, some scholars such as al-Jahiz (d.869) warned against over-emphasis of memorisation as a pedagogical tool due to its negative impact on independent thinking. For al-Jahiz:

> The leading sages, masters of art of deductive reasoning and [independent] thinking were averse to excellence in memo-risation, because of [one's] dependence on it and [its rendering] the mind negligent of rational judgment, so [much

so] that they said: 'memorisation inhibits the intellect.' [They were averse to it] because the one engaged in memorisation is only an imitator, whereas deductive reasoning is that which brings the one engaged in it to calculated certainty and great confidence.

(Cited in Gunther 2006:372)

Finally, the correct method and manner of teaching children was also a focal point in many philosophical and educational discussions. In addition to ethical conduct, piety, and critical thinking, nurturing the creative spirit of children was also discussed by classical Muslim thinkers. For example, as early as the ninth century, Ibn Sahnun (d.870), who was born in al-Qayrawan, not far from Ibn Khaldun's birthplace in north-central Tunisia, published a book called the *Rules and Conduct for Teachers*, a useful treatise on curriculum, pedagogy, and disciples. In a lengthy discussion, he provides sound advice relating to nurturing creative faculties in children in order to challenge their minds (Gunther, 2006).

## Educational Pedagogy and the Qur'an

Ibn Khaldun's views on education and pedagogy covered both elementary and higher education. In fact, he gave considerable attention to discussing the right attitude and the proper method of instruction required for teaching, as failure to adopt the correct method of teaching could significantly impact the learning of the students. The key method of instruction should be to gradually introduce a subject to students and to ensure that they do not leave with the impression that scholarship is difficult. Ibn Khaldun states how too often:

> We have observed that many teachers of the time in which
> we are living are ignorant of this effective method of teach-
> ing. They begin their instruction by confronting the stu-
> dent with obscure scientific problems. They require him to
> concentrate on solving them. They think that that is expe-
> rienced and correct teaching, and they make it the task of
> the student to comprehend and know such things. In actual
> fact, they (merely) confuse him by exposing him to the final
> result.
>
> (Ibn Khaldun, 1958, Vol.3: 293)

Ibn Khaldun's ideas were shaped by three factors: Firstly, the broad literature on a range of disciplines including the religious and philosophical sciences, and secondly, his personal observations based on his extensive travels throughout North Africa and Andalusia. Ibn Khaldun was particularly interested in exploring how Islamic studies was taught in different locations throughout the Muslim world. Finally, Ibn Khaldun's views on education were informed by his own education and tutelage under his teacher and mentor, Al-Abili.

Regarding the education of children, age is an important factor in the nurturing of character. According to Ibn Khaldun, teaching and learning the Qur'an should be part of early years' education, because of 'the desire for the blessing and reward (in the other world resulting from the knowledge of the Qur'an) and a fear of the things that might affect children in "folly of youth" and harm them and keep them from acquiring knowledge' (Ibn Khaldun, 1958, Vol.1: 304–305). Failure to teach children at a young age may result in them missing the chance to learn the Qur'an. As long as children are young and remain at home, Ibn Khaldun argues, they are amenable to authority. But, when they have grown up and 'shaken off the yoke of authority, the tempest of young manhood often casts them upon the shores of wrongdoing. Therefore, while the children are still at home and under the yoke of authority, one seizes the opportunity to teach them the Qur'an, so that they will not remain without knowledge of it' (ibid). It is important for children to be taught the Qur'an from an early age, as this determines the spiritual condition of the learner.

The teaching of the Qur'an was universal throughout the regions Ibn Khaldun visited, so much so that teaching children the Qur'an was considered to be an important 'symbol of Islam'. He argues that 'Muslims have, and practise, such instruction in all their cities, because it imbues hearts with a firm belief (in Islam) and its articles of faith, which are (derived) from the verse of the Qur'an and certain Prophetic traditions' (Ibn Khaldun, 1958, Vol.1: 300). It is the central pillar of Muslim education because it orientates people towards the centrality of life and its purpose. The teaching of the Qur'an, given its critical importance to Muslim lives and society, becomes the bedrock for other disciplines. It is also the springboard through which all habits are nurtured and directed. For Ibn Khaldun, the teaching of the Qur'an is the foundation from which everything else is taught. The justification for this is provided in the following observation:

> The Qur'an has become the basis of instruction, the foun-
> dation of all habits that may be acquired later. The reason
> for this is that the things one is taught in one's youth take
> root more deeply (than anything else). They are the basis of

(all) knowledge. The first impression the heart receives is, in a way, the foundation of (all scholarly) habits. The character of the foundation determines the condition of the building.
(Ibn Khaldun, 1958, Vol.1: 300–301)

Ibn Khaldun was intrigued by the different approaches and regional variations in teaching methods across the Muslim world. For example, the characteristic feature of Maghribi or North African education is 'to restrict the education of the children to instruction in the Qur'an and to practice, during the course (of instruction)' (Ibn Khaldun, 1958, Vol.3: 301). Within the system the educators will 'not bring up any other subjects in their classes, such as traditions, jurisprudence, poetry or Arabic philology, until the pupil is skilled in it' (ibid.). This approach is problematic because the child fails to receive a rounded education of the ancillary subjects associated with Qur'anic studies. Despite such reservations, Ibn Khaldun notes how through this method of learning, students develop a depth of knowledge of the correct *tajwid* or Qur'anic orthography by heart. The above approach to Qur'anic studies is contrasted with the Andalusian method, which is grounded in a system that focuses on the breadth of ancillary disciplines associated with the Qur'an, including Arabic language, poetry, and handwriting. Judging by Ibn Khaldun's language in the following extract, it is clear that he sees the Andalusian model as an effective way of teaching children.

The Spanish method is instruction in reading and writing as such. That is what they pay attention to in the instruction (of children). However, since the Qur'an is the basis of and foundation of (all) that and the sources of Islam and (all) the sciences, they make it the basis of instruction, but they do not restrict their instruction of children exclusively to (the Qur'an). They also bring in (other subjects), mainly poetry and composition, and they give children expert knowledge of Arabic and teach them good handwriting. They do not stress teaching of the Qur'an more than the other subjects... He then has some experience and knowledge of the Arabic language and poetry. He has an excellent knowledge of handwriting, and he would have a thorough acquaintance with scholarship in general.

(Ibn Khaldun, 1958, Vol.3: 301)

Ibn Khaldun's suggestion for a more contextual approach to learning is based upon the premise that a child needs to make sense of the Qur'an by considering the Arabic language, the historical context and the principles of jurisprudence associated with Islam. In many respects, some of the main concerns associated with teaching the Qur'an to non-native Arabic students is that children will be learning the Qur'an without an understanding of its meanings and how it relates to everyday life. For Ibn Khaldun, it is thoughtless,

[of] our compatriots in that they teach children the Qur'an when they are first starting out. They read things they do not understand and work hard at something that is not important for them as other matters... The student should study successfully the principles of Islam, the principles of jurisprudence and the prophetic sciences connected with them.

(Ibn Khaldun, 1958, Vol.3: 304)

In response to this concern, Ibn Khaldun provides an interesting response by drawing upon the writings of Abu Bakr

b. al-Arabi (d.1148), the famous Andalusian Maliki judge, and the author of the *Rihla*. According to Ibn al-Arabi, 'Poetry and Arabic philology should be taught first because of the existing corruption of the language.' Once the child has a good understanding of Arabic and poetry 'the (student) should go to arithmetic and study it assiduously, until he knows its basic norms. He should then go to the study of the Qur'an, because with his previous preparation it will be easy for him' (Ibn al-Arabi, cited in Ibn Khaldun, 1958:304). Despite this sound advice, Ibn Khaldun demonstrates how people may be reluctant to make effective changes to the educational system, especially given how norms of teaching can often eclipse the finer points of pedagogy. Ibn Khaldun endorses the above advice by Ibn al-Arabi but is quick to accept how customary norms may not be favourable to it, considering how custom holds great power over forces of change.

## Chapter 3

# *Reason and Faith: Approaches to the Study of History*

**T**hroughout the history of Islam, philosophers and theologians have devoted considerable attention to understanding the nature of God. To avoid matters of doubt and conflict, some theologians have been content to be guided by faith and revelation. Some have even argued that matters of faith should take priority over reason, even where it appears to be irrational. For those advocating a theological worldview, the ultimate *truth* is grounded in the Qur'an, hadith traditions and the scholarly consensus *(ijma)* of the Muslim community. However, the critically-minded philosophers reject such a position; instead they maintain that both reason and revelation, properly understood, can lead people to the Divine. Whatever concessions made by the theologians to the philosophical approach 'it never ceased to hold to the primacy of the religious law over reason—the philosophers, on the other hand, the order was the reverse: they upheld the primacy of rational enquiry in both the theoretical and the practical sciences' (Mehdi, 1957:36–37).

Whilst some scholars are fixed on Ibn Khaldun's rationalist worldview, focusing on the influence of the Greek rationalist tradition in general and the Islamic Platonist traditions in his thought (Mahdi, 1957), others have noted some tensions within the *Muqaddimah* between the rationalist aspects and the mystical elements (Irwin, 2018). Indeed, these tensions at the core of Ibn Khaldun's work should be seen as both original and complex—Ibn Khaldun was a Sufi who was willing to support all kinds of obscurantism to defend the cause of his religion (ibid.), while at the same time laying claim to the great heritage of rationalist philosophy. The apparent contradiction should not be seen as 'absurd, static or paralyzing opposition between two irreducibly antagonistic attitudes, but with a contradiction that was both dialectical and productive' (Lacoste, 1984:193). Despite the scholarly dispute over his work, it should be noted that Ibn Khaldun does argue like a 'modern scientist'. The questions he poses are similar to those we are now asking and the causes he uncovers in his magnum opus are of interest to contemporary scholars. Indeed, it is Ibn Khaldun's modern scientific attitude that distinguishes him from most other scholars of the classical period (ibid.).

The above discourses on reason and religion are a product of political and intellectual history. To understand

Ibn Khaldun's position on this matter, one must have an understanding of key events that shaped the intellectual history of the Muslim world. This chapter aims to provide a broad historical overview of the relationship between philosophy, theology, and political rule. It will show how the translation movement during the Abbasid period led to the transmission of key texts on philosophy, medicine and science into the Arabic language; this had a major impact in merging the scientific and philosophical understandings of previous civilisations with an Islamic worldview. The second section of this chapter will explore the role of reason in Ibn Khaldun's approach to studying history. For Ibn Khaldun, the importance of studying history is located in the critical analysis of source materials together with the uncovering of the laws of history. The final section of this chapter attempts to contrast Ibn Khaldun's approach to rational thought with Islamic mysticism, and in doing so, locates Ibn Khaldun as a complex and multi-faceted scholar. More crucially, it sees these elements of apparent contradictions as productive and dialectical.

## Faith and Reason: A Historical Context

The formative period of philosophy within the Muslim world was during the Abbasid period (750–1517), which began with the crushing defeat of the Umayyad Empire. The 'Golden Age' associated with early Abbasid rule was marked by great economic prosperity, strong centralised government, and the rise of a remarkable civilisation renowned for its scholarship. The development of Islamic legal systems which began under Umayyad rule was supported and nurtured under the

Abbasids. In fact, by the eighth century the scholars formed a distinctive social class, symbolised by their authority in the Qur'an, hadith, and religious law (Makdisi, 1981). The scholars would come to represent piety and hope. They would go on to argue that human life 'should be directly under the guidance of God's laws, and anything in society not clearly necessary to His service was to be frowned upon' (Hodgson, 1974:238).

In addition to the flourishing of Islamic theology, the Abbasid caliphate witnessed the rise of Islamic philosophy, literature, medicine, art, and sciences. The expansion of the Muslim empire throughout the world allowed non-Arab speaking populations to enter into the fold of Islam, with Arabic shifting from the language of the Arab people to gaining a unique status within literature and public discourse (Esposito, 1994). As the Islamic empire expanded, the Muslim scholarly imagination sought to understand and not reject knowledge systems from former civilisations such as Greek, Indian and Chinese.

The translation of Greek philosophical and scientific writings into Arabic began during the peak of the Abbasid era. The translation movement is often associated with Caliph al-Ma'mun (d.833). It is claimed that after meeting the philosopher Aristotle (d.322 BC) in a dream, he was deeply inspired by Greek and Hellenistic sciences. Whilst al-Ma'mun is often credited for the famous translation centre, Bayt al-Hikma (House of Wisdom), translation activities had already begun under Caliph al-Mansur (d.755). The role of Bayt al-Hikma in the dissemination of scientific knowledge was critical, especially in philosophy and medicine. By the end of the translation movement in the tenth century, a staggering range of scientific and philosophical texts by Greek scholars had been rendered into Arabic [via Syriac] by Muslim and Arab Christian scholars, such as Hunayan Ibn Ishaq (d.873). The translation of key texts include the mathematical works of Euclid and Ptolemy and medical writings of Greek authorities, especially the works of Galen (Adamson 2016:20). This allowed Muslim scholars, such as al-Razi (d.925), al-Farabi (d.950), Ibn Sina in particular, (d.1037), al-Biruni (d.1048) and Ibn Rushd (d.1198), to play an instrumental role in the scholarly community by reconciling Hellenistic heritage with the teachings of Islam. This period showcased the intellectual brilliance of these scholars. This can be seen in the following biographical reflection of Ibn Sina:

> I busied myself with the study of the *Fusus al-Hikam* [a treaty of al-Farabi] and other commentaries on physics and mathematics, and the doors of knowledge opened before me. Then I took up medicine... Medicine is not one of the difficult sciences, and in a very short time, I undoubtedly excelled in it, so that physicians of merit studied under me. I also attended the sick and the doors of medical treatments based on experience opened before me to an extent that cannot be described. At the same time, I carried on debates and controversies in jurisprudence. At this point I was sixteen years old.
>
> (Lewis, 1974 cited in Esposito, 1984:55)

The socio-cultural transformation of this period would have a profound impact on all Abrahamic faiths. Muslim thinkers would go on to influence a range of scholars; most significantly, the Jewish philosopher and the influential Torah scholar, Moses Maimonides (d.1204) and the Christian philosopher, theologian and jurist, St. Thomas Aquinas (d.1274). In fact, the greatest irony is that Muslim philosophers such as Ibn Rushd would have more influence on Jewish and Christian thinkers than Muslim intellectuals (Leaman, 1993:769). This period also shaped a distinctive rationalist scholar, dedicated to a worldview based upon reason, science, and learning. The rationalists were interested in religion, but equally interested in all aspects of nature, knowledge of the self (medicine, psychology), society, and the cosmos. The ideal person for the rationalist was a *philosopher* dedicated and committed to reason and truth, so that the individual could be in harmony with life. This is further explained:

> Given this rational knowledge of the first principles of nature, and of himself, everything else followed from the Philosopher, both his personal manner of life and his conception of how society as a whole should be ordered. The more nearly a person could approach to such rationality, the more nearly he could fulfil his own purpose in existence and be in harmony with all life. For the *Faylasuf*, the ideal man was a sage 'philosopher'—a man who fully lived up to the demands of the tradition of Philosophia.
>
> (Hodgson, 1974:418)

The success of this movement was only made possible through the political support it received by some Abbasid caliphs. The rational approach to religion through the Mu'tazilite doctrine, which gives precedence to the role of reason in understanding the nature of God, was given political legitimacy by Caliph al-Ma'mun and others. Ironically, the theological rationalism of the Mu'tazilites also led to the *Mihna* or religious persecution of scholars who did not conform to rational theology. The rise and subsequent decline of this reason-based theological worldview is captured succinctly in the following:

> The intellectual awakening took the country by storm. It seized the imagination of all intellectuals, the philosophers, the rationalist theologians, and traditionalist jurist consults. Before it took its hold on law, however, it was used as a weapon by the rationalist theologians against the adherents of traditionalism during the Inquisitions [or *Mihna*]. The Mu'tazilite theologians had secured the support of Caliph al-Ma'mun and after him al-Mu'tasim... They sought to force upon the traditionalists their rationalist doctrine... But their efforts ended in failure. The *Mihna* went down in Islamic history as the initial triumph of traditionalism.
>
> (Makdisi, 1981:79–80)

## History as an 'Extraordinary Science'

In the *Muqaddimah*, Ibn Khaldun was adamant that he was developing *al-ulum al-gharib* or 'extraordinary science', a unique philosophically informed way of interpreting historical events. He was keen to reject the claim that the study of history is solely determined by events of the past; rather, he argued for an approach to history which includes an analysis of the underlying significance of historical events. For Ibn Khaldun, historical insight 'requires *nazar*, philosophical speculation, a product of speculative intelligence, the third and highest level of reasoning Ibn Khaldun describes... on human thought' (Dale, 2015:152).

In stressing the importance of history, Ibn Khaldun makes a crucial distinction between those who grasp the surface level meaning of history, which serves to inform and entertain the masses, and those who aspire for a much deeper 'inner' understanding of the philosophy underpinning historical events. According to Ibn Khaldun, the former understanding of history is located within the ignorant masses; only the learned can grasp the latter.

> For on the surface history is no more than information about political events, dynasties and occurrences of the re-mote past, elegantly presented and spiced with proverbs. It serves to entertain large, crowded gatherings and brings to us an understanding of human affairs. It shows how changing conditions affected (human affairs), how certain dynasties came to occupy an ever-wider space in the world, and how they settled the earth until they heard the call and their time was up.
>
> (Ibn Khaldun, 1958, Vol.1: 6)

Ibn Khaldun is deeply sceptical of recycled myths by those with very little understanding of history as a specialist discipline. He warns against those who propagate false rumours and gossip as history; this is particularly pertinent given how the study of history is often politicised or silenced by various governments to meet political ends. Ibn Khaldun (1958, Vol.1: 6–7) finds Muslim historians without proper training and qualification concerning, because the history introduced in their books consists of either freely invented gossip or discredited reports. Many of their 'successors followed in their step and passed that information onto us as they heard it. They did not look for, or pay any attention to, the causes of events and conditions, nor did they eliminate or reject nonsensical stories' (ibid).

Perhaps the most important factor which undermines the study of history is the blind imitation of tradition, what Ibn Khaldun calls the 'pasture of stupidity', which can only be overcome by developing a critical eye. Blind faith in tradition is not an isolated problem when it comes to the study of history; rather, it is a major problem which Ibn Khaldun attributes to leading Muslim historians. The stature of Ibn Khaldun's scholarship allows him to make a critical assessment of the approaches to history adopted by a range of towering Muslim historians, such as the historian, geographer and traveller al-Masudi (d.956). Ibn Khaldun was highly critical of al-Masudi, the 'Herodotus of the Arabs', due to his transmission of historical events without critical assessment or scrutiny of historical information. The true study of history, according to Ibn Khaldun, should transcend the elementary and surface level description of history, which reduces the past to mere historical events. One should rather ponder and reflect upon the significance of these events or indeed aspire to understand the laws of history. This can only happen through a detailed analytical interpretation of key events. The inner meaning of history involves critical thinking aimed at a systematic [re] interpretation of historical events, which inevitably involves finding answers to the how and why of events. In short, the study of history, for Ibn Khaldun, is so critical that it should be considered a branch of philosophy (Dale, 2015).

Ibn Khaldun's mission was to present an alternative methodology for writing history. This was partly motivated by the concern that his fellow historians were not scrutinising and critically examining the source material or the contents passed down through the generations. We are reminded how,

> the later historian was all tradition-bound and dull of nature and intelligence, or, (at any rate) did not try not to be dull. They merely copied (the older historians) and followed their example. They disregarded the changes in conditions and in the customs of nations and races that the passing of time had brought about... Their works, therefore, gives no explanation for it. When they then turn to the description of a particular dynasty, they report the historical information about it (mechanically) and take care to preserve it as it had been passed down to them, be it imaginary or true.
>
> (Ibn Khaldun, 1958, Vol.1: 9)

In response to the problems associated with the science of historiography (the study of history and of its written histories), Ibn Khaldun presents a more critical and rational approach to the science of history. He makes a useful contribution to rational ways of dealing with historical facts and establishing how and why dynasties and civilisations originate. Ibn Khaldun is mindful of the fact that his study is subject to geographical location; in other words, it is restricted to the North African experience and to the Arab/Berber experience. Ibn Khaldun's approach to the study of history is further explained as follows:

> In (this book) I lifted the veil from conditions as they arise in the various generations. I arranged it in an orderly way in chapters dealing with historical facts and reflections. In it I showed how and why dynasties and civilisations originate...

in the work, I commented on civilisation and urbanisation, and on the essential characteristics of human and social organisation, in a way that explains to the reader how and why things are as they are and shows him how the men who constituted a dynasty came upon the historical scene. As a result, he will wash his hands of any blind trust in tradition. He will become aware of the conditions of the periods and races that were before his time and that will be after it.

(Ibn Khaldun, 1958, Vol.1: 11)

It is clear from Ibn Khaldun's writings that he aimed to understand the complex and contradictory nature of society. In fact, he aimed to develop a global conception of history by analysing the evolution of the socio-political nature of society. In doing so, Ibn Khaldun was able to demonstrate how each of these complex events are governed by logical principles (Lacoste, 1984).

Ibn Khaldun (1958) maintains that history encompasses information about social organisation, which he argues is 'identical with world civilisation.' It is governed by conditions affecting the nature of civilisation, which includes a range of complexities from 'savagery and sociability, group feelings and the different ways by which one group of human beings achieves superiority over another' (Ibn Khaldun, 1958, Vol.1: 71). Furthermore, history also covers the wider political issues governing the nature of 'royal authority and the dynasties that result in this manner and with the various ranks that exists within them' (ibid.). Finally, it covers various activities and occupations which act as a social glue, including 'sciences and crafts that human beings pursue as part of their activities, and with all the other institutions that originate in civilisation through its very nature' (ibid.). It is the rational explanation for the socio-political turmoil which allowed one empire to be replaced by another.

## Method of *Thinking* Historically

Some academics like to present Ibn Khaldun as a unique rationalist scholar who provided many insights into the human condition. They locate Ibn Khaldun's views on knowledge, reason, and religion within the Greco-Islamic tradition (Dale, 2015). Indeed, the first volume of the *Muqaddimah* presents a strong rationalist case by criticising the descriptive and hagiographical accounts of history as presented by various Muslim scholars. Ibn Khaldun's view of history aims to develop the 'correct' method of studying the past. He mentions in the foreword to the *Muqaddimah* how the subject of history is widely cultivated among various nations. However, he is particularly concerned by the way ordinary people aspire to know history, when very few people can grasp the significance of this specialist discipline.

Ibn Khaldun's *Muqaddimah* is considered a masterpiece not because of the rational and analytical manner in which he viewed human history and society, but because he was the first to depart from the traditional method which viewed history through a set of predictable clichés and events based upon exaggerated superstitions. For Ibn Khaldun, the secret to understanding the past lies beyond the chronicles of dates and events to much broader explanations of ideas. As such, the Khaldunian method was one of the earliest attempts, based on logical and scientific approach, of the study of human society. In doing so, he warns historians not to conflate the 'essence' of a given society with accidents of history. In order to guide the historian, Ibn Khaldun developed a logical way of approaching the subject matter. The historian should have the capacity to clearly distinguish 'truth' from fiction; this is achieved by critically analysing records and historical scholarship as a way of assessing the essence of a particular society. Furthermore, Ibn Khaldun encouraged students of history to ask deeper questions, such as: do the historical records state logical truths? Are the reports exaggerated? While Ibn Khaldun lists several philosophical and scientific skills required to make sense of history, a summary of these is noted below:

> Know the principles of politics, the... nature of existent things, and the difference among nations, places, and periods, with regards to ways of life, character qualities, customs, sects, schools, and everything else. He further needs a comprehensive knowledge of present conditions in all these respects. He must compare similarities and differences between the present and the past conditions in all these respects. He must compare the similarities or differences between the present and the past... conditions. He must know the causes of similarities in certain cases and the differences in others. He must be aware of the differing origins and beginnings of... dynasties and religious groups, as well as reasons and incentives that brought them into being and circumstances and history of the persons who supported them.
>
> (Ibn Khaldun, 1958, Vol.1: 55–56)

Perhaps the most crucial element of the skill set that Ibn Khaldun lists is the fundamental goal of the scholar to combine rational knowledge of the nature of society with empirical research (Dale, 2015:157). This is clearly articulated in the final segment of the above observation by Ibn Khaldun, when he states that a given scholar must have 'complete knowledge of the reasons for every happening and to be acquainted with the origin of every event. Then, he must check transmitted information with the basic principles [of nature and accidental] he knows' (Ibn Khaldun, 1958:56). Furthermore, Ibn Khaldun reminds the reader that sociology, or the study of society, is a crucial discipline for any historian. For Ibn Khaldun, the secret is to think historically by looking at the bigger picture, especially when it comes to understanding, explaining and thinking through problems of the present. 'History' is not simply the study of the past, but rather lessons and principles inherited from the past that are crucial in making sense of the present. Influence of the Khaldunian approach can be found in several contemporary thinkers, such as the philosopher of science Jerry Ravetz (2021:104): 'In my own struggles with, and writing on science, going back well over six decades, I have attempted to think historically. Roughly, that means understanding the conflicts of the present in terms of the unresolved contradictions inherited from the past.'

## Faith [in] Allah and Faith [in] Reason

Epistemology, or the branch of philosophy that deals with the central question of how reality is known, was a key topic of debate throughout the classical period of Islamic civilisation. Whilst Ibn Khaldun was not a conventional philosopher he nevertheless had the necessary training to engage in philosophical debates and take strong positions on key philosophical issues of the day. The classical period of Islam witnessed an ambivalent, at times hostile, relationship with philosophy. Many, such as al-Ghazali (1997) in *The Incoherence of the Philosophers*, felt that early Greek philosophy had undermined the principles of Islamic creed or *aqeedah*. The task of *The Incoherence* was simply to refute the philosophers (especially al-Farabi and Ibn Sina) by showing the inherent contradiction in their theories. He states how the philosophical beliefs and 'the contradiction of the metaphysical statements, relating at the same time their doctrine as it actually is, so as to make it clear those who embrace unbelief in God through imitations that all significant thinkers, past and present, agree in believing in God and the last day' (al-Ghazali, 1997:xxii). A few writers disagreed with al-Ghazali's approach, especially Ibn Rushd, who wrote a famous response titled *The Incoherence of the Incoherence*.

Whilst Ibn Khaldun recognised the importance and the role of philosophy, he qualified this by stating that students should only engage with logic and related principles of philosophy after they have mastered the religious sciences. This, as articulated below, is due to the potential harm and negative impact studying philosophical matters may have on a person's religious faith.

> One knows what harm it can do. Therefore, the student of it should beware of its pernicious aspects as much as he can. Whoever studies it should do so (only) after he is saturated with the religious law and has studied the interpretations of the Qur'an and jurisprudence. No one who has no knowledge of the Muslim religious sciences should apply himself to it. Without that knowledge he can hardly remain safe from its pernicious aspects.
>
> (Ibn Khaldun, 1958, Vol.3: 257–258)

Ibn Khaldun's view on philosophy was shaped by prominent Muslim thinkers such as Ibn Rushd, especially in recognising two essential paths to knowledge: reason and revelation. In other words, Ibn Khaldun did not see any contradiction between affirming knowledge based upon revelation, and equally recognising the validity of reason, especially when it came to examining the external world of politics and society. Ibn Khaldun argued that Islam demands uncritical submission and 'faith in' Allah; rational faculties cannot be relied upon to understand Allah, because immaterial forces cannot be proven by logical proofs. However, he did not completely reject the role of the intellect in faith and revelation. He did this by maintaining the Ash'arite position, which recognised the need to defend the tenets of religion with logical proofs. For example, he drew upon logical arguments and theology to dismiss a range of disciplines, especially the validity of astrology, by using on both hadith literature and Greek philosophy to question how stars can influence human fate. However, he does maintain the importance of 'faith in' reason, which demanded the critical study of the natural and material world. In short, 'he rejected the idea that reason trumped faith when it came to acquiring the knowledge of the divine... philosophy prevailed over faith when it came to explaining the dynamics of North African and even Arab political history' (Dale, 2015:75).

### Three Degrees of the Intellect

Ibn Khaldun reminds his readers that the first principles of tackling epistemological problems require 'human action in the outside world', which 'materializes only through thinking about the *order of things*, since things are based upon each other' (Ibn Khaldun, 1958, Vol.2: 415). He argues how crucial it is to appreciate a sequence of events as well as how they are connected to each other, especially between what is evolving on a global scale with what is happening on a local scale. For Ibn Khaldun, critical thinking is paramount, as it distinguishes men from the animal kingdom. He states that 'it should be known that God distinguished man from other animals by an ability to think which He made the beginning of human perfection and the end of man's noble superiority over existing things' (Ibn Khaldun, 1958, Vol.2: 411). He goes on to mention how humans are unique due to their rational faculties to *perceive* (Ibn Khaldun defines perception as consciousness) things outside their essence by using the ability to think. Ibn Khaldun draws pedagogical lessons from his epistemological framing of knowledge and argues that teachers should aim to nurture the rational faculties of their students with the ability to see events beyond their surface level appearance. For Ibn Khaldun, our ability to think has three degrees—each of these provide practical pedagogical tools for educators.

The first degree is 'man's intellectual understanding of things that exist in the outside world in a natural or arbitrary order, so that he may try to arrange them with the help of his own power' (Ibn Khaldun, 1958, Vol.2: 412–413). He goes on to point out how this form of intellect, which he defines as 'discerning intellect', can be used to gain things which are useful to their livelihood and to shun things that will bring about any harm (ibid.). The second degree or 'experimental intellect' includes one's ability to think with ideas, experiences and appropriate behaviours needed in dealing with others.

This 'mostly conveys apperceptions, which are obtained one by one through experience, until they have become really useful' (ibid.). The third degree includes the speculative intellect, which provides hypothetical and theoretical knowledge of things that require no practical activity and go beyond sense perception. The aim of speculative intellect is to 'provide with the perception of existence as it is with its various genera, differences, reasons and causes. By thinking about these things, (man) achieves perfection in his reality and becomes pure intellect and speculative soul' (ibid.). Ibn Khaldun adds that the combination of the three forms of intellect, leads to 'pure intellect' and true understanding of human reality.

Ibn Khaldun (1958, Vol.3: 284–287) further elucidates seven aims of literary composition. In other words, students or scholars engaged in scholarly endeavours should aim to fulfil one or more of the following objectives; failure to do so exposes ignorance and impudence. Although Ibn Khaldun was writing in the fourteenth century, all of the points listed below are key objectives within modern academic scholarship also.

1. The *invention* of new science
2. To provide new *interpretation* to existing knowledge
3. To offer *corrections* to existing ideas
4. To *perfect* any existing disciplines which may be incomplete
5. *Improvement* of a particular science
6. Literary *criticism*
7. *Abridgment* of ideas

## Politics, *Ulama* and the Rational State

Ibn Khaldun's writings were not restricted to history and education. They also included analysing the role of politics within the 'rational state' (Dale, 2015). For Ibn Khaldun, the Rashidun Caliphate, or the four 'rightly guided' caliphs, modelled the ideal type of political rule. This is because the nature of their political rule was not aimed towards personal gain, but rather devoted to a system which aimed to serve the spiritual, social, and political needs of the community. After the Rashidun Caliphate, there was a marked change in political objectives. Ibn Khaldun notes how the Umayyad Caliphate (660–750) and the subsequent rise and decline of the Abbasid Dynasty (750–1517) led to a pre-occupation with luxury and worldly pleasure. Moreover, with the rise of independent sultanates from the tenth century, a new period of political rule prevailed, one which marginalised the influence of religious scholars or *ulama*. Ibn Khaldun maintained that in light of the significant changes in society, the skills that the scholars possessed were no longer needed. For example:

> Alluding to *ulama* complaints that they, the rightful 'heirs of the Prophet', as Muhammad is reported to have described, were wrongly excluded from royal councils, Ibn Khaldun says they are wrong to imagine they should influence sultanate regimes, thus continuing the critical roles they had played in the caliphate. The sultan's monarchical authority was not derived from divine law; rather it issued from the 'nature of society and human existence... The nature of society', he continued, 'does not require that jurists [*muftis*] and scholars [*ulama*] have any share (in authority).
>
> (Dale, 2015:213)

79

The above observation does not deem the role of the *ulama* redundant, but confines the scholars to the domain of 'religion' and not the rational politics of the state. Furthermore, it is argued that the inclusion of scholars within the domain of the state carried more symbolic value rather than a meaningful state role. The sultans regularly honoured the scholars and jurists, not only as an act of kindness, but also due to their 'high regard of Islam and their respect for men who are in any way concerned with it' (Ibn Khaldun, 1958, Vol.1: 460). As is clearly highlighted below, the scholars continued to receive respect and reverence from the sultans, but this did not mean that they had any executive powers to administer.

> Their position in the dynasty derives from the fact that (the dynasty) takes care of the Muslim religious community... They have no standing in the dynasty because they are honoured as personalities. Their standing merely reflects an affection of respect for their position in the royal councils, where it is desired to make a show of reverence for the religious ranks. They do not have any executive authority to make decisions (in these councils). They are merely used as authorities on religious law, and their decisions (*fatwa*) are accepted. This is indeed the fact. God gives success.
>
> (Ibn Khaldun, 1958, Vol.1: 459)

The bracketing of any executive powers from the religious clergy was not motivated by animosity towards the *ulama*, but because the skills involved in running the politics of the state are too complex and contradictory. The state was prepared to regularly consult them on religious matters, but 'advice on political matters is not their province, because they have no group feeling and do not know the conditions and laws which govern' (Ibn Khaldun, 1958: 460). Ibn Khaldun's view of religious leaders was informed by his own observations in Cairo during the end of his life. He felt that their ethical standards had been compromised due to their proximity to the Sultans. This can be seen when some of the *ulama*, used to luxurious perks, were motivated to teach the children of the nobility, rather than students from the lower class of society. As a result, their group solidarity (or *asabiyya*) with the general masses was weakened, which is directly opposite to the ranks of the noble companions of the Prophet during the rule of the Rashidun caliphate (Dale, 2015).

## Rational Thinker and Sufi

Ibn Khaldun is not a name one typically associates with Sufism, especially given his reluctance in sharing his personal ideas on spiritual matters (Ozer, 2017). In fact, there has been a conscious attempt by various academics to see Ibn Khaldun as a positivist (scientific) thinker; in doing so, they reject Ibn Khaldun's association with Islam, let alone Sufism. For example, as early as the nineteenth century the Austrian politician and orientalist Alfred von Kremer (d.1889), who held several very important political roles within Beirut's and Cairo's colonial history, viewed references to religion in the *Muqaddimah* as carrying a symbolic and stylistic function (ibid.). In the twentieth century, the Egyptian writer and intellectual Taha Hussain (d.1973), who wrote on Ibn Khaldun's philosophy, viewed the *Muqaddimah*, especially its ideas on the rise and fall of civilisation, as being void of any religious or theological explanation (see Chapter 4). Ibn

Khaldun was a complex scholar whose thinking juxtaposed a reason-based worldview within an esoteric worldview; his rational approach was shaped by his teacher Al-Abili, whilst his father played a critical role in shaping his religious and spiritual view of life. It is clear from his *al-Ta'rif*, or autobiography, that both his father and grandfather retired from a career in politics to devote themselves to a quiet, contemplative life in Sufi Zawiyas in Tunis. The socio-political context of the times in which Ibn Khaldun was living was also very crucial in shaping his ideas on mysticism. For example, some of the previous dynasties within North Africa, such as the Almoravid (see Chapter 1) were critical of Sufism, while the Marinid dynasty, which ruled North Africa during the time of Ibn Khaldun, were avid defenders of Sufism (Ozer, 2017).

More crucially, Ibn Khaldun's ideas on Islamic mysticism can be found within his *Muqaddimah*; however, the translation of Ibn Khaldun's *Shifa al-Sa'il li-Tahdhib al-Masa'il*, or *Remedy for the Questioner in Search of Answers* by Yumna Ozer (2017) provides useful insights into his views. The *Shifa* does not take the form of a spiritual manual as it is a treatise on the critical debate within fourteenth century Andalusia on whether mystical travellers can depend on writings found in books or whether they require oral teachings from a spiritual master. In the *Shifa*, Ibn Khaldun maintains the premise that students must have spiritual teachers; he does this through denouncing 'the Sufis who compiled books in which they tried to describe with technical words some mystical truths that no books could possibly contain, and no words could possibly express because spiritual realities go beyond the limits of conventional language' (Ozer, 2017:xxx). For Ibn

Khaldun, Sufism began with the call to Islam, and the Prophet Muhammad (saw) along with his companions were the first Sufis. As such, it cannot be separated from the essence of Islam (Ozer, 2017). More crucially, Ibn Khaldun was also critical of certain types of Sufi practices, developed throughout the Muslim world which are 'contaminated by pure unbelief and vile innovations' (Ibn Khaldun cited in Morris, 2009:249).

There are no references within the *al-Ta'rif* that Ibn Khaldun underwent any spiritual initiation under the guidance of any spiritual master; nevertheless, some commentators have argued that Ibn Khaldun may have been a member of the Shadhili Tariqa. This claim is justified by the fact that Ibn Khaldun was buried in Makbarat al-Sufiyya, Egypt—the resting place for Shadhili Sheikhs—and the dominance of the Shadhili Order throughout North Africa and Egypt (Ceyham, 2008:486).

## Chapter 4

# Ibn Khaldun, Asabiyya and the Rule of Four

**A**ny student of history or an informed traveller will be familiar with the great achievements of former civilisations. He or she will also note the complex and multi-faceted history of Islam as captured in *Beyond Timbuktu: An Intellectual History of Muslim West Africa* by Ousmane Oumar Kane, or *The Legacy of Muslim Spain*, edited by Salma Jayyusi. In fact, the richness of Muslim history throughout the Abbasid Dynasty, Ottoman Empire, Mughal India and beyond is symbolised through its diverse tapestry crystallised in art, architecture, scholarship and science. It is not only Islamic societies that produced civilisations. Great civilisations are discussed within the Old Testament, and Greek and Roman history is the mainstay of much classical education and schooling in the West. The multi-volume *Science and Civilisation in China* by Joseph Needham charts the complex history of China, and the three-volume *Black Athena* by Martin Bernal further questions the Eurocentric premise of Western civilisation.

Ibn Khaldun was more than familiar with ancient history and well-versed in Islamic history. For Ibn Khaldun, as highlighted in Chapter 3, the role of the scholar is not to simply document history as a series of events, but rather, the critical challenge is to look beyond the surface level of these events. In looking at the regional history of North Africa, such as the Almoravids, Almohads and the competing struggles between the Hafsid and Marinid dynasties, Ibn Khaldun was attempting to answer a crucial question: what causes the rise and fall of civilisations and empires? This chapter will explore Ibn Khaldun's theoretical ideas in understanding the nature of this phenomenon. Although his view was restricted to the North African context, several scholars have attempted to use the principles of Ibn Khaldun's ideas as a way of understanding world history (Alatas, 2015).

The central concept of the Khaldunian worldview is *asabiyya*. Some writers find the concept difficult to translate and have failed to capture the essence of what Ibn Khaldun was trying to convey by it. The English translation of the *Muqaddimah* uses 'group feeling' within and between people to convey the meaning of *asabiyya* (Rosenthal, 1958). A range of commentators used other synonyms to capture the essence of *asabiyya*, including: 'sense of solidarity', 'group feeling', 'group loyalty', 'esprit de corps' (Rabi, 1967:49), 'group consciousness' (Daood, 1967:xii) and 'group cohesion, and common will' (cited in Laborde,1984:101). In short, *asabiyya* can be seen as a set of attitudes and emotions governed by complex social processes which have psychological ramifications. It is an old concept which is derived from the Arabic root word *-s-b*, meaning to 'bind or tie together' (Lacoste, 1984:103). The word in fact appears in hadith literature, as the following example illustrates: 'A companion of the Prophet asked, "Does *asabiyya* mean loving one's people?" "No," replied the Prophet, "*asabiyya* means helping one's people in just action" (ibid).

Ibn Khaldun explained the rise and fall of civilisations through the transformation of two distinct ways of living, namely rural *(umran badawi)* and urban *(umran hadari)*. When Ibn Khaldun wrote about *asabiyya*, he had in mind the bond or the feelings of social solidarity that hold empires and civilisations together. In fact, Ibn Khaldun was not the first person to use the concept of *asabiyya*; it was used within pre-Islamic societies to indicate a 'kind of common cause with one's agnates, which might lead to blind support of one's group without regard for justice of its cause' (Rabi, 1967:3–4). For example, Ibn Khaldun noted how within rural *(badawi)* societies, *asabiyya* emanates from three distinct kinds of relationship, namely blood ties, alliance and clientship (ibid). The social context of many rural societies, especially when it comes to issues such as protection against external threats, means that *asabiyya* based upon blood and tribal kinship is crucial for survival, which is why there is an emphasis on purity of lineage and compassionate feelings based upon common descent. Focusing on blood ties, Ibn Khaldun writes:

> Respect for blood ties is something natural among men, with the rarest exceptions. It leads to affection for one's relations and blood relatives (feeling that no harm ought to befall them, nor any destruction come upon them... It makes for mutual support and aid, and increases the fear felt by the enemy... This strengthens their stamina and makes them feared, since everybody's affection for his family and his *asabiyya* is more important (than anything else).
>
> (Ibn Khaldun, 1958, Vol.1: 264)

Conversely, in urban societies new types of reciprocal social actions emerge, as life within new towns surrounded by the protection of the city wall gives its population different forms of protection. Ibn Khaldun notes how people from rural societies gradually adapt to urban life. To start off with, rural forms of *asabiyya* based upon kin are gradually replaced by new and more 'governmental measures... to replace the power of tribal chiefs' (Rabi, 1967:52).

Following the inception of Islam, the 'blind loyalty' to tribe or kin, regardless of ethical principles or cultural bias, began to be challenged. In response to this, Ibn Khaldun's idea of *asabiyya* was re-interpreted within the prism of Islamic ethics. He argued that *asabiyya* based upon religion had the capacity to embed powerful feelings of solidarity and unite communities against evil intents and jealousies. This was particularly critical given the expansion of Islamic empires and the mixing of Arabs and non-Arabs whilst sharing a common religion and value system.

The related concept to Ibn Khaldun's analysis is the cyclical nature of history. Ibn Khaldun's detailed observations on political life enabled him to reject a linear understanding of history. Instead, he developed a cyclical view of history, based upon the comparative idea of human nature: that empires, underpinned by sovereignty and political power, can be compared with all living organisms—they are born, mature, decline and perish.

## Ibn Khaldun and the Political Nature of Man

At the centre of the Khaldunian worldview is the idea that both geography and history play a critical role in shaping people's character and appearance. A universal trait is that social beings are created to live, and to achieve greatness through collective action. Ibn Khaldun's concept of 'man', and by extension, women, runs contrary to the main philosophical position rooted in the Western concept of 'individualism', which maintains that an individual should be free to learn and to discover ideas which serve the interest of the self, and not the presumed interest of the tribe, social group or society at large. In fact, it is impossible for humankind to organise everything deemed necessary to survive without the cooperation of fellow humans. For Ibn Khaldun, the highest achievement of any collective group is its ability to build, develop, and sustain civilisation. The process of transcending injustice and barbarity and achieving civilisational goals can be summarised as follows:

> Full co-operation results in the complicated social process of 'urbanisation'. Hence the dictum 'Man is political by nature', i.e., he needs the kind of social organisation in order to satisfy his material and other requirements. But, because man is an animal, proper order among men co-operating in such social organisation can exist only when they are governed by justice in the form of a retraining influence that

keeps them from devouring each other... As soon as social organisation is formed, civilisation (*'umran*) results. The Arabic word, derived from a root, means 'to build up, to develop'.

(Rosenthal, 1958, Vol.1: xl)

As an astute historian, Ibn Khaldun understood the nuances associated with the remarkable civilisations produced under the banner of Islam. As a trained Maliki theologian, he was more than familiar with the Qur'anic (3:110) reminder: 'You have become the best community ever raised up for mankind, enjoining the right and forbidding the wrong, and having faith in God.' Moreover, as a keen historian he was equally acquainted with the historical reality of how seriously Muslims throughout the ages took the above Qur'anic prophecy. In doing so, they attempted to recast the history of the world by developing a complex civilisation in accordance with the above verse, soon after the start of the Prophetic message:

> Muslims succeeded in building a new form of society, which in time carried with it its own distinctive institutions, its art and literature, its science and scholarship, its political and social forms, as well as its cult and creed, all bearing an unmistakable Islamic impress. In the course of centuries, this new society spread over widely diverse climes, throughout most of the Old World. It came closer than any had ever come to uniting all mankind under its ideas.
>
> (Hodgson, 1974:71)

The complicated social process for developing civilisation and governing justice is called *asabiyya* or group solidarity. No civilisation can form or survive without it. In fact, the power of *asabiyya* is so paramount that it can determine the rise and fall of dynasties. According to Ibn Khaldun, all dynastic rule is mortal; but unlike human mortality, dynastic rule goes through a process of cyclical changes. Each of these changes determine the rise, growth, decline, death and subsequent re-birth of the state. Ibn Khaldun sees the rise of dynastic rule often carrying the seeds of its own downfall; this happens when conflict emerges between rulers of given dynasties, with its amalgamation of power and wealth, and the *asabiyya* of the people within its political domain, which is crucial to sustain the state. When this inevitable conflict manifests itself, the rulers often impose more taxes on the population to recruit external support at the expense of internal group solidarity. This is clearly articulated in the following:

> [the] bias towards luxury, however, carries with it the seeds of the dynasty's eventual decay and disintegration. The desire of the ruling group to gain exclusive control over all the sources of power and wealth brings about a conflict between the dynasty and the men whose *asabiyya* sustains it. Its members thus resort to military support from out-side sources; and in order to raise the money necessary for this purpose (and for their luxuries) they impose more and more taxes. Gradually the dynasty loses its grip on the reins of power, with the ruler becoming a ruler in name only, controlled by some outsider who is not a member of the dynasty.
>
> (Ibn Khaldun, 1958:xlii)

Ibn Khaldun maintained that humans are essentially a product of their social environment; their future is determined by the wider social bonds that they create and nurture. Ibn Khaldun's understanding of group dynamics is influenced by the classical Muslim perspective of 'man' as understood by Ibn Sina and others. This is based upon the idea that human beings do not have the ability to accomplish all the things that are necessary for their livelihood, unless they have full co-operation of others. Even if this were possible, argues Ibn Khaldun, it would be very difficult and problematic. Thus, it is both pertinent and necessary for mutual support within the spirit of collective action, for the functioning of the local economy and the development of trade, commerce and nurturing of creative talents. In short, Ibn Khaldun argues social action is necessary for intellectual perfection and for the improvement of the human condition within this world and the next. This is clear in the following summary Ibn Khaldun provides, quoting al-Shahrazurd:

> He would not be able to obtain the various kinds of intellectual perfection (that are the goal of humanity). Thus, of necessity there must exist a group the members of which co-operate to acquire many different crafts and (technical) skills. In this way, each individual accomplishes something from which his fellow men can profit. (The sages) said 'man is political by nature' in the sense that he needs this kind of social organization in order to live, to provide for his own livelihood, to improve his situation in this world, and to perfect his soul for the next world... The proper order of such social organization is political and based upon cooperation.
>
> (Cited in Ibn Khaldun, 1967:xxiv–lxxv)

Several scholars have pointed out how Ibn Khaldun's ideas were informed by his own sociological and empirical observations (Schmidt, 1930). He grounded his classification of human societies in his own detailed observations of culture, institution, habitat and, most importantly, group solidarity. From this, he was able to develop a sociological theory to understand the impact of social factors in shaping human behaviour. This unique approach to sociology was based upon his 'applying empirical procedure to social phenomena'. In doing so, Ibn Khaldun introduced a new approach in this field of study. His 'inclination to devote his works to facts and realities of life was clear in the task he assigned to himself, i.e., to reveal the nature of human association as it is and not as it ought to be whether according to proposed rules of ethics, religion, or wisdom' (Rabi, 1967:28).

The methodological approach underpinning the study of *asabiyya* is essentially based on a 'scientific methodology' which emphasises the need to gather 'facts' to understand social reality, rather than follow hearsay or received wisdom passed down through generations. As we have already seen, this is clear from a detailed reading of the *Muqaddimah*. For example, Ibn Khaldun dismisses the works of several leading Muslim historians because they place 'blind trust in tradition' which undermines scrutiny and academic rigour with 'little effort made to get at the truth' (Ibn Khaldun 1958:5–9). In this respect, Ibn Khaldun is a committed social scientist interested in understanding his socio-political environment, based upon social realities and free from any moral judgments. This is confirmed by various academics who have suggested that 'one of the interesting traits of Ibn Khaldun... is the extent to which he is a sociologist rather than a moralist' (Gellner, 1981:86). More crucially, his relationships with political rulers were based on technical advice regarding 'points of detail, or on the wisdom of knowing things... he indulged in no preaching' (ibid).

## Ibn Khaldun and Group Dynamics

Contemporary discourse on group dynamics is usually associated with negativity or hostility; a quick survey of the perception of group dynamics within the black (Hall 1978; Gilroy 2004) or Muslim community (Alexandra 2000, Miah, 2015) reveals how both groups have been associated with hyper-masculinity and gang culture respectively. In fact, this follows a particular trend in the study of group dynamics within social psychology. As early as 1896, Le Bon (1896) discussed the idea of the 'group mind' to refer to the way in which groups carry a 'collective mentality', which allows them to act in irrational ways (cited in Brown 2000). In addition, some academics have argued that group behaviour enables individuals to carry out crimes such as riots and revolutions, because it allows members to separate individualised actions through a 'cloak of anonymity' (ibid.).

More recently, social psychologists have also confirmed the above observation, by demonstrating how group behaviour or any form of group unity grounded upon common, mutual, or collective purpose or action have often received negative press. They argue that group behaviour is often associated with 'social un-desirable aspects: de-individualisation, prejudice, social loafing and group think, rather than more positive aspects of team spirit, intergroup cooperation, group productivity and collective problem solving' (Brown, 2000:xiv). Contrastingly, the Khaldunian imagination of *asabiyya* sees group cohesion not only as highly desirable, but also as natural and essential for any civilisation (From hertz, 2011). Ibn Khaldun's idea, as already noted in Chapter Three, encompasses a classical Islamic worldview, which is supported by a number of traditions attributed to the Prophet Muhammad (saw), such as the oft-quoted authentically collected sources: 'stick to the group and beware of being separate' and 'the group is a mercy and separation is torment'. For Ibn Khaldun, *asabiyya* provides a source of social identity; it plays a crucial role in defining the way people conceptualise their world and, most importantly, how the 'out-group' is perceived. Ibn Khaldun further articulates the importance of group solidarity by drawing upon the famous story of Prophet Joseph and his brothers in the Qur'an:

> They said to their father: 'If the wolf eats him, while we are a group, then, indeed, we have lost out'. This means that one cannot imagine any hostile act being undertaken against anyone who has his group feeling to support him.
>
> (Ibn Khaldun, 1958, Vol.1: 263)

## Asabiyya and the Rule of Four

Ibn Khaldun's theory is based on the understanding that history is not simply the study of, or the understanding of, the past; rather, history has a constant present. Current social norms, values and political ideas are shaped by historical forces, which not only inform the present but also shape the future. As several contemporary scholars have pointed out, the 'ever present historical memory provides a source of cultural identity, social cohesion, a sense of permanence amid change and a means of rejuvenating the present and shaping the future' (Sardar, 1998:131).

For Ibn Khaldun (1958), human beings are essentially a product of their social environment. They were created to live together in communities, as part of a wider social network. He argues that they are unable to maintain a fulfilling life on their own. Given the fact that humans are rational beings, it is not surprising to note that individuals live together in groups to achieve their basic needs and fulfil their higher socio-political objectives through *asabiyya*. For *asabiyya* to flourish, four distinct kinds of relationship are central, namely, blood ties, alliance, clientship and religion. Each of these relationships play a crucial role in protecting individuals within the group (Rabi, 1967).

The concept of *asabiyya* is also critical when it comes to defending against external threats and attack. For Ibn Khaldun, the defence and protection of communities is determined by group solidarity; he notes how safeguarding and security can only be successful 'if they are close knit groups of common descent. This strengthens their stamina and makes them feared, since everybody's affection for his family and his group is more important than anything else' (Ibn Khaldun, 1958, Vol.1: 263) Ibn Khaldun further notes that a successful form of *asabiyya* generates fear and at the same time commands respect from other people. For Ibn Khaldun (1958, Vol.1: 273), fear and respect can be generated through religion (as in the case of the Abbasid Empire). To elaborate this point, he introduces the idea of 'house'. The fear and respect of groups is based upon the principle of 'house', which means that an individual is able to count people of nobility and great standing among their extended family and ancestors. The fact that 'he is their progeny and descendant give him great standing among his fellows, for his fellows respect the great standing and nobility that his ancestors acquired through their qualities' (Ibn Khaldun 1958, Vol.1: 273).

In addition to family kinship, Ibn Khaldun (1958) considered religion a crucial element of *asabiyya*. For him, 'group feeling is necessary to the Muslim community. Its existence enables (the community) to fulfil what God expects of it'. Religious solidarity along with numerical support of citizens is equally crucial in maintaining political support. This is clear from the following:

> The expansion and power of a dynasty correspond to the numerical strength of those who obtain superiority at the beginning of the rule. The length of the duration also depends on it. The life of anything that comes into being depends upon the strength of the temper. The temper of dynasties is based upon group feeling... Group feeling, in turn, depends on numerical strength.
>
> (Ibn Khaldun, 1958, Vol.1: 331)

The above observation also demonstrates the importance of *asabiyya* in the formation of the state. Ibn Khaldun's idea on state formation can be contrasted with the view of al-Farabi found in his seminal text, *On the Perfect State*. This declared that any successful ruler of a given state should be a philosopher, or at the very least the ruler should be advised by philosophers. Al-Farabi's ideas on the perfect state, informed by high ethics, were strongly influenced by Greek thinkers, especially the works of Plato.

For Ibn Khaldun, this approach to state formation was highly ambitious, grounded in utopian vision and lacking awareness of the complex nature of state formation. Ibn Khaldun's view was empirical and more pragmatic as it recognised the political and social structures of society. He witnessed how the historical development of state formation took into consideration two essential distinctions between nomadic and sedentary groups. Strong *asabiyya* rooted in *umran badawi* or nomadic life would gradually lead to movements of people towards *umran hadari* (sedentary life) or life in the towns. This is because only nomadic tribes had strong group solidarity to establish states. The 'solidarity born out of rigours of nomadic life enabled their chieftains to conquer and found empires. The stability of the state was based upon the solidarity that united its founder' (Lacoste, 1994:92). *Asabiyya* within this context would suggest giving birth to new forms of living. Gradually, this group becomes comfortable with wealth and luxury and becomes sedentary. They become cowardly, weak and preoccupied with the trappings of their wealth and comfort. In doing so, they slowly lose their military strength and group solidarity. As a result, they become 'weaker and less united, they become incapable of preserving cohesion of the tribe... Another nomadic tribe closer to the rigours and isolation of desert life would then defeat them' (ibid.).

This cycle of stronger tribes moving from the desert to the cities and replacing existing weaker groups was seen to repeat itself every four generations. The first generation of Bedouins moving from nomadic life to the cities are loyal to their group and see success through group solidarity and cohesiveness. It is *asabiyya* that gives success, sustenance and political legitimacy, and the rulers ensure that the qualities that lead to their success are at the centre of their priorities. For Ibn Khaldun (1958, Vol.1: 278–279), the first generation are 'the builders of the family's glory [and] they know what it costs [them] to do the work, [they] keep the qualities that created his glory and made it last'. The second generation still has association and loyalty to the group and puts in place the relevant support systems to nurture the rule of the founding fathers. Ibn Khaldun notes how the son and other family members that come after the father have 'personal contacts with his father and thus learned those things from him. However, he is inferior to him in this respect, inasmuch as a person who learns things through study is inferior to a person who knows them from practical application' (ibid.).

Discord and dissent start to emerge within the third generation. This is when rulers begin to enjoy the luxuries of dynastic rule and lose contact with the group by employing external experts. This reliance on external support instead of utilising group solidarity, group cohesion and tradition leads to further weakening of *asabiyya*. For Ibn Khaldun, the 'third generation must be content with imitation and in particular, with reliance upon tradition. This member is inferior to him of the second generation, inasmuch as a person who relies upon traditions is inferior to a person who exercises independent judgment' (ibid.). Finally, the fourth generation falls victim to new, stronger forces of *asabiyya* emerging from nomadic societies. The process then repeats itself. This is because the fourth generation,

> is inferior to the preceding ones in every respect. Its member has lost the qualities that preceded the edifice of its glory. He despises (those qualities). He imagines that the edifice was not built through application and effort. He thinks that it was something due to his people from the very beginning by virtue of the mere fact of their descent, and not something that resulted from the group (effort) and individual (qualities). For he sees the great respect in which he is held by the people, but he does not know how that respect originated... He keeps away from those in whose group feeling he shares, thinking that he is better than they. He trusts that (they will obey him because) he was brought up to take their obedience for granted and he does not know what qualities that made obedience necessary.
>
> (Ibn Khaldun, 1958, Vol.1: 279–280)

It is clear that all great civilisations and political dynasties, similar to humans, are mortal just as the world of the elements and all it contains comes into being and decays (Ibn Khaldun, 1958). So, group cohesion, tradition and culture through the laws of nature go through similar modification. Society, by its nature, goes through transition and change which, according to Ibn Khaldun, is usually (but not always) underpinned by the rule of four generations. The rule of four (generations) with respect to prestige usually holds true. 'It happens that a "house"' is wiped out, disappears and collapses in fewer than four, or it may continue unto the fifth and sixth generations, though in a state of decline and decay' (Ibn Khaldun, 1958, Vol.1: 277).

## Asabiyya: Social, Political and Ethical Force

Following the same scholarly tradition, one particular study has assessed the impact of *asabiyya* as having three distinctive features, namely: *asabiyya* as a social force, *asabiyya* as a political force and *asabiyya* as an ethical and moral principle (Rabi, 1967). Whilst this study is rather dated, it nevertheless allows Ibn Khaldun's ideas to have contemporary relevance by considering the sociological and ethical dynamics within the concept of *asabiyya*.

### Asabiyya as social force

The central tenet of *asabiyya* is based upon a social bond between people of shared kinship or cultural ties. The social bond, with its emphasis on fellowship, partnership, and association, gives energy and momentum to group solidarity. Moreover, the inevitable power of association, affiliation and attachment to the group is crucial for its strength and longevity (Ibn Khaldun, 1958). Ibn Khaldun viewed group solidarity as a product of the social environment, playing a vital, tenacious, and powerful function, first in rural communities then in urban societies. This point is reinforced by the following:

> Its function as a social bond and a coordinating power is, then, an attribute of a particular stage of group development which again proves one of the assumptions reached in discussing Ibn Khaldun's method. That is to say, that his analysis shows a tendency in favour of giving priority to the same way of living, as an important factor in determining the shapes, circumstances, and roles of *asabiyya*.
>
> (Rabi, 1967:67)

*Asabiyya* acts as a force of unity and consensus for group dynamics; it also helps by providing the group in question with clear objectives and a sense of direction. In fact, *asabiyya* as a social force has two distinctive objectives. Firstly, 'it nurtures solidarity and vigour within one's own group because of the aforementioned ties; secondly, it unites people by mere force, to compromise the conflicting *asabiyyas*, to form one great and powerful group' (Rabi 1967:65). Ibn Khaldun argues that the absence of coordinated cooperation and group solidarity may give rise to disintegration, internal division, and discord between groups, which often leads to bloodshed and violence.

## Asabiyya as political force

The concept of *asabiyya* can be viewed as a vehicle for political action. It has already been argued that it is a driving force for history, and most importantly, the mechanism through which the fates of empires and political dynasties are determined (Fromhertz, 2011). More crucially, the *Muqaddimah* has led one leading scholar to recognise the intricate relationship between the practice of *asabiyya*, the nature of power and Islamic ideology (Lawrence 1984). Moreover, it has shown how *asabiyya* is principally a vehicle that is used to 'establish political power either within limited groups or over the whole community' (Rabi, 1967:61). All political action encompasses a principle, cause or a set political objective that a group hopes to achieve. *Asabiyya* plays a crucial role in achieving these objectives through the process of group solidarity. Moreover, during times of political upheaval, *asabiyya* can play a vital function in defending the group against external forces by reinforcing and stabilizing the influence of religion within the group.

The success of the political demands made by groups is largely determined by the harmony, consensus, and cohesion of those groups. If the *asabiyya* is strong and versatile, the group is likely to be successful in achieving the desired political goals or objectives. One of the key aspects of achieving political goals is the idea that strong *asabiyya* will enable the group in question to state certain claims and demands. Ibn Khaldun, in the following observation, further reinforces this point:

> ... group feeling produces the ability to defend oneself, to of-
> fer opposition, to protect oneself and to press one's claim...
> people whose group feeling cannot for its own defend them
> against oppression certainly cannot offer any opposition or
> press any claims.
>
> (Ibn Khaldun 2005:111)

### Asabiyya as moral value

Two types of *asabiyya* can be noted—the pre-Islamic and Islamic forms. The pre-Islamic concept of *asabiyya* is based upon blind, unconditional support for a group, which often meant carrying out actions without due regard for ethical considerations or the 'justice of its cause' (Rabi 1967:49). For Ibn Khaldun, pre-Islamic forms of *asabiyya* are a product of *jahiliyya*, or pre-Islamic ignorance, which is antithetical to the Islamic worldview (Lings, 1998). The pre-Islamic acts of *jahiliyya* are contrasted with Ibn Khaldun's understanding of the primordial nature of humans, who are innately inclined towards righteousness. This is summarised by the following:

> In view of his natural disposition and his power of logical
> reasoning, man is more inclined towards good qualities than
> towards bad qualities, because the evil in him is the result of
> the animal powers, and inasmuch as he is a human being, he
> is more inclined towards goodness and good qualities.
>
> (Ibn Khaldun, 1958:291)

The principle that Ibn Khaldun uses to navigate between
pre-Islamic and Islamic ideas of *asabiyya* is judged by its
objectives or consequences of human action; the exercise of
power and the pronouncements of group feelings of solidarity
should be determined by their objectives (Rabi, 1967). If
these are conducted in compliance with religious principles
associated with the common good or even meaningful secular
objectives, then *asabiyya* is acceptable. It has been further
concluded that 'in this way, Ibn Khaldun was able to utilise
the idea of *asabiyya*... to differ categorically and purposefully
from those reflected by the old tradition. It is in this sense that
his idea of *asabiyya* can be considered as a constructive moral
concept' (Rabi 1967:68).

# *Conclusion*

Ibn Khaldun was a profound scholar, thinker and polymath. His contributions to diverse scholarly fields such as economics, education, history, philosophy, and sociology had a major influence on Western scholarship. Ibn Khaldun's writings represent a comprehensive synthesis of social sciences achieved by classical Muslim scholars. In doing so, his works provide the modern, non-specialist reader a glimpse into the eclectic and original thinking of the Muslim world. This brief introduction to Ibn Khaldun's life and works in the field of education, history, and sociology aims to place him alongside the pantheon of other Muslim luminaries such as Ibn Sina, Al-Ghazali, Ibn Rushd and non-Muslim thinkers such as the Greek historian Thucydides, Italian political strategist Machiavelli, and sociologists such as Comte, Durkheim, and Marx.

European interest in Ibn Khaldun's writings was in part ignited by colonial expansionist aims. The sociology of Muslim societies combined with Ibn Khaldun's theoretical ideas, which explained the rise and fall of Muslim societies, was of great interest to French colonial administrators. Ibn Khaldun was first known to the Western world through the early seventeenth century Latin translation of Arabshah's biography of Tamerlane, which discusses the historical meeting between Ibn Khaldun and the Mongol conqueror (see Chapter 1). Further interest in Ibn Khaldun amongst European scholars came though the Ottoman polymath Katib Celebi's (d.1657) bibliographical work, titled *Kashf al-zanun*. Celebi, described as the 'greatest encyclopaedist amongst the Ottomans', served the basis of the French orientalist Barthélemy d'Herbelot de Molainville's (1695) *Bibliothèque Orientale*, which is considered to be the first Western encyclopaedia of the Islamic world.

In the early nineteenth century, Ibn Khaldun further attracted the interest of the French linguist Silvestre de-Sacy, which resulted in a partial translation of Ibn Khaldun's *Muqaddimah* (published in 1810) under the title *Histoire des Berberes* (History of the Berbers). According to many observers, this translation is considered to be the greatest textual event in the history of French Orientalism. It was de-Sacy's student, William de-Slane, who would be commissioned by the French government to catalogue important books in the libraries of North Africa. De-Sacy would also complete the translation of the *Muqaddimah* between 1862 and 1868.

The *Muqaddimah* was translated into multiple European languages. As early as 1922, sections of it were included in Nicholson's translation of *Eastern Poetry and Prose*. Charles Issawi's brief translation of the *Muqaddimah* was later published in 1950 under the title *An Arab Philosophy of History*. This translation includes a useful introduction to Ibn Khaldun's ideas on education, history, economics, society and philosophy. Eight years later, the complete version of Ibn Khaldun's *Muqaddimah* was published by Franz Rosenthal; this translation from the Arabic includes a very detailed introduction to Ibn Khaldun's life together with a comprehensive textual history of the *Muqaddimah*. A popular abridged and edited version of the Rosenthal translation was completed by N.J. Dawood with an introduction by Bruce Lawrence as part of the Princeton University Press Bollingen Series.

Whilst scholars of the Arabic language broadly welcomed the translation of the *Muqaddimah* in the English language, it nevertheless attracted criticism based on its technical and idiomatic aspects. For example, George Makdisi (1961:59) questions the quality of Arabic translation, together with Rosenthal's ability to capture the technical ideas and subtle nuances of Ibn Khaldun's key concepts.

> The principal merits of his works are to be found in the introduction to the translation and in the annotation, both of which are of highest quality. But the translation leaves much to be desired... Aside from the questionable renditions into English with which some Arabist will justly have cause to disagree... the translation suffers from excessive 'doctoring' consisting mainly in the chopping of Ibn Haldun's sentences into smaller independent units. The inevitable result is a text which, at best, is only remotely reminiscent of Ibn

Haldun. The Arabist familiar with Ibn Haldun cannot fail to sense this alienation in spirit between text and translation.

The role of knowledge production in the translation movement was indispensable to the French colonial administration of North Africa. In order 'to know the natives, one had not only to observe them, study them, and understand their culture and their society, but also to know their past' (Hannoum, 2003:61). Thus, the aim of the translation of key texts from the classical Islamic period in the French language demonstrates how knowledge is regulated by power; in doing so, local knowledge of culture, religion and custom is transformed into colonial knowledge (Said, 1978). It is crucial to note that the focus on Ibn Khaldun during this period was not to understand his ideas of history or philosophy, but rather 'the officers of the Arab Bureau, the military institution that assured both the production of knowledge and the establishment of order, were mainly ethnographers, with little concern for history' (Hannoum, 2003:61).

The colonial use of Ibn Khaldun's work by Orientalist scholars is not the only legacy of Western scholarship. It is equally worth recognising the intellectual influence Ibn Khaldun had on European scholars and writers. For example, Charles Issawi (1950:2) in his partial translation of the *Muqaddimah* in the English language states how 'it is not too much to say that Ibn Khaldun is the greatest figure in the social sciences between the time of Aristotle and that of Machiavelli and as such deserves the attention of everyone who is interested in these sciences.' He goes on to note how 'more than any of his contemporaries, whether European or Arab, he tackles the kind of problem which preoccupies us today,' namely, the nature of society, role of education and learning.

As early as 1893, Robert Flint, author of *The History of Philosophy of History*, devoted significant space to Ibn Khaldun. He starts by recognising how Ibn Khaldun was one of the first scholars 'to treat history as the proper object of a special science' (Flint 1893:157). The historian Philip K. Hitti (d.1978) echoes the above point by stating Ibn Khaldun was 'one of the greatest historians and philosophers ever produced by Islam and one of the greatest of all time' (cited in Lacoste 1984:1). The philosopher and anthropologist Ernest Gellner (1981:86) would go a step further and make use of Ibn Khaldun's ideas alongside the works of Emile Durkheim in his classical text, *Muslim Societies* (1981). He praised Ibn Khaldun's methodological approach to studying society; for Gellner, one of the 'interesting traits of Ibn Khaldun... is the extent to which he is a sociologist rather than a moralist: modern sociologists may preach *Wertfreiheit,* he practised it.'

*Wertfreiheit* is a methodological tool developed by the German sociologist Max Weber (d.1920) to refer to the importance of recognising and reducing one's personal bias in research. Gellner (1981) further notes that when Ibn Khaldun 'offers advice to princes, it is basically technical advice on points of detail, or on the wisdom of knowing things for what they are: but when it comes to the basic features of the social system, he indulges in no preaching' (ibid).

Gellner (1981) was not the only social scientist to recognise Ibn Khaldun's 'modern' sociological approach. Indeed, one of the key skills that are nurtured within contemporary universities is the ability to conduct research without personal bias. Ibn Khaldun's 'greatness as a philosopher and historian' was a product of his unique methodology and commitment to his discipline—this is very clear from his approach to the study of religion within the non-Islamic world, especially the study of Zoroastrianism, Judaism and Christianity. The issue concerning modern scholars of Ibn Khaldun is not the breadth of Ibn Khaldun's writings dealing with non-Muslim subject matter, but rather his objective approach to the study of the sources, which included Muslim, and more critically, non-Muslim sources. In fact, Ibn Khaldun's methodological approach to Zoroastrianism, Judaism, and early church history, shows how:

> [Ibn Khaldun] as an orthodox Muslim, could detach himself from the fetters of his own faith and penetrate into the theological and doctrinal differences of another religion. Indeed, amongst the Arab-Muslim scholars who attempted such a study, it was Ibn Khaldun, the great Muslim thinker of the fourteenth century, who achieved astounding scholarly objectivity in regards to the various non-Islamic religions.
>
> (Fischel, 1967:137)

The breadth and scope of Ibn Khaldun's interest in non-Islamic and more crucially pre-Islamic communities might come as a surprise, especially given his observation: 'My intention is to restrict myself in this work to the Maghreb, the circumstances of its races and nations, and its subjects and dynasties, to the exclusion of any other regions' (Ibn Khaldun, 1958, Vol.1: 52). His interest in non-Muslim communities was largely shaped by his time in Egypt, which prompted a 'thorough and systematic investigation of the Islamic, as well as the non-Islamic East' (Fischel, 1967:111). Ibn Khaldun's (1958, Vol.1: 12) change of heart in studying his non-Muslim subjects was due to his scholarly inquisitiveness. He notes how 'later on, there was my trip to the East... in order to study the systematic works and times on [Eastern] history. As a result, I was able to fill the gaps in my historical information.' Ibn Khaldun's natural curiosity about the non-Muslim world was also shaped by the classical Islamic genre of travel literature. His close and often critical stance on the historian, traveller, and prolific writer al-Masudi (d.956) further sparked his interest. Al-Masudi was a keen traveller who was interested in Muslim and non-Muslim societies—he visited all of Asia, including China, India and Ceylon. Indeed, al-Masudi was not the only historian and traveller interested in non-Muslim societies; Ibn Fadlan (d.960) a contemporary of al-Masudi, witnessed and wrote about Viking burials, and the renowned polymath al-Biruni (d.1050) born seventeen years after the death of al-Masudi, examined the Hindu faith in his classical text *Tarikh al-Hind* (History of India).

Ibn Khaldun's methodological approach to his subject matter was also unique for several reasons. First, his approach combined and integrated different sources without due regard for the author's religion, ethnicity, or political affiliation; he would often put them all on an equal footing. Second, Ibn Khaldun scrutinised his source materials; he would always compare and verify statements in a rigorous and methodical way, highlighting their contradictions, divergences, and omissions. Finally, when comparing the historical and genealogical data, he would comment: 'this is far from the truth,' 'this is not correct,' 'this is contradictory,' and 'this is impossible' (Fischel, 1967:119). Considering the above points regarding Ibn Khaldun's methodological approach, combined with his development of social theory as a way of explaining the social realities of North Africa, led many leading sociologists to accept him as a precursor to modern sociology. For example, the sociologist Ludwig Gumplowicz (d.1909) described Ibn Khaldun as 'a sociologist of the fourteenth century' (for a detailed discussion on this topic see, Schmidt [1930]).

It was the British historian Arnold J. Toynbee (1975) and author of the twelve volumes *A Study of History* that further elevated the status of Ibn Khaldun within Western scholarship (Irwin, 1997). It is important to note that Toynbee's transmission of Ibn Khaldun's theory of history is crucial, 'for, until the appearance of Franz Rosenthal's translation, Toynbee did more than anyone else to popularize Ibn Khaldun's theories to the English-speaking world' (Irwin 1997:466). Toynbee was deeply influenced by Ibn Khaldun's cyclical understanding of historical events. He further described Ibn Khaldun as an Arab genius, whose works can be compared with any of the Western canonical figures, included Thucydides, Vico and Machiavelli. Regarding Ibn Khaldun's 'Universal History' Toynbee states how 'he has conceived and formulated a philosophy of history which is undoubtedly the greatest work of its kind that has ever yet been created by any mind in any time or place' (Toynbee, 1934). It wasn't only Western academics who recognised the remarkable abilities of Ibn Khaldun. The Andalusian polymath and poet Ibn Khatib (d.1374), a friend and contemporary of Ibn Khaldun, described his scholarly credentials in the following:

[Ibn Khaldun] was a man of virtue, combining all finest qualities; highly esteemed and rock-solid in repute; reserved in assemblies, high-minded and steadfast; exceptional in both the intellectual and narrative arts; many faceted, rigorous researcher, possessed of a prodigious memory, forthright in his concepts, skilled in penmanship, and wonderful company-in sum, veritable paragon of the Maghribi region.

(Ibn al-Khatib, cited in Himmech, 2004:17)

In contemporary universities most academic disciplines tend to be studied separately; each of these subjects have their own core reading and most of the time, scholars within each subject rarely engage in critical dialogue. Ibn Khaldun was perhaps one of the earliest thinkers to recognise the importance of interdisciplinary approaches as a way of understanding complex social realities. In his attempt to understand the nature and development of society, he provided the historian with rational methods of assessing the past based upon a close examination of historical records. For Ibn Khaldun, the 'past resembles the future as water resembles water' (cited in Issawi, 1950:7); in other words, the study of society (or the present) is informed by the study of the past. In short, history supplies the materials for sociology. In fact, the study of society is a golden thread weaving throughout the *Muqaddimah* and his *Universal History*. For example, in Book I of the *Muqaddimah*, Ibn Khaldun highlights a general overview of sociology. In Book II and III he discusses the importance of sociology and politics. A detailed discussion of sociology of urban life and sociology of economics is discussed in Books IV and V. Finally, sociology of knowledge takes prominence in Book VI.

The Eurocentric bias of positioning Western theorists and academics at the centre of intellectual universe, whilst pushing Muslim or non-European thinkers to the fringe, is an important topic addressed by Professor Syed Farid Alatas. Alatas (2014) is seen as a leading expert on the works of Ibn Khaldun, who has devoted his life to bringing the sociological works to a contemporary audience. In his book *Applying Ibn Khaldun: The Recovery of a Lost Tradition in Sociology,* he makes a compelling case for a shift away from seeing Ibn Khaldun as a founder or precursor of modern sociology to a movement which embraces his theoretical perspectives by successfully integrating concepts from his writings into modern sociological theories. In this approach, Ibn Khaldun is not situated in the past, but rather located among contemporary thinkers and theorists who continue to make significant contributions to academic disciplines in the present.

# Bibliography

Abdulganiy, O., Olamilekan, A. A. (2019). The Legacy and Legendary of Ibn Khaldun as a Fore-Runner Scholar in Sociology. *International journal of social sciences & educational studies, 5*(3), 128–141.

Abdullahi, A. A., & Salawu, B. (2012). Ibn Khaldun: A Forgotten Sociologist? *South African review of sociology, 43*(3), 24–40.

Adamson. P. (2016) Philosophy in the Islamic World. Oxford: Oxford University Press

Ahmed, A. (2005) Ibn Khaldun and Anthropology. The Failure of Methodology in the Post 9/11 World. *Contemporary Sociology.* 34 (6), pp. 591–596.

Ahmed, Z. (2003) *The Epistemology of Ibn Khaldun.* New York: Routledge.

Alatas, S.F. (1990) Ibn Khaldun and the Ottoman Mode of Production, *Arab Historical Review for Ottoman Studies.* 1 (2), pp.45–63.

Alatas, S. F. (2006). Ibn Khaldun and Contemporary Sociology. *International sociology, 21*(6), 782–795.

Alatas, S. F. (2006). A Khaldunian Exemplar for a Historical Sociology for the South. *Current sociology, 54*(3), 397–411.

Alatas, S.F. (2012) *Ibn Khaldun.* Oxford: Oxford University Press.

Alatas, S.F. (2014) *Applying Ibn Khaldun: The Recovery of a Lost Tradition.* London: Routledge.

Alexandra, C. (2000) *Asian Gangs.* Oxford: Berghahan.

Al-Azmeh, A. (2012). *Ibn Khaldun: A Reinterpretation*: Taylor and Francis.

Al-Azmeh (1981) *Ibn Khaldūn in Modern Scholarship: A Study in Orientalism.* London: Third World Centre for Research.

Al-Ghazzali (1988) *The Book of Knowledge.* New Delhi: International Islamic Publishers.

Al-Ghazzali (1998) *The Incoherence of the Philosophers.* Brigham Young University.

Al-Masudi (2007) *The Meadows of Gold.* London: Penguin.

Attar, S. (2007) *The Vital Roots of European Enlightenment. Ibn Tuffayal's influence on Modern Western Thought.* Plymouth: Lexington Books.

Baker, O. (1998) *Classification of Knowledge in Islam: A Study in Islamic Philosophies of Science.* London: Islamic Text Society.

Bennison, A. (2016) *The Almoravid and Almohad Empires.* Edinburgh: Edinburgh University Press.

Brown, R. (2000) Group Process: Dynamics Between and Within Groups. Oxford. Blackwell.

Ceyhan, S. (2008). Ibn Khaldun's Perception of Sufis and Sufism: The Discipline of Tasawwuf in Umran, *Asian Journal of Social Science, 36* (3-4), 483-515.

Dale, S.F. (2015) *The Orange Trees of Marrakesh: Ibn Khaldun and the Science of Man.* Harvard: Harvard University Press.

Enan, M.A. (1993) *Ibn Khaldun: His Life and Work.* Lahore (India): Sh. Muhammad Ashraf.

Esposito, J. (1994) *Islam the Straight Path.* Oxford: Oxford University Press.

Enan, M.A. (1993) *Ibn Khaldun: His Life and Work.* Lahore (India): Sh. Muhammad Ashraf.

Fakhry, M. (2002) *Al-Farabi: Founder of Islamic Neoplatonism.* Oxford: One World Press.

Fischel, W.J. (1967) *Ibn Khaldūn and Tamerlane: Their Historic Meeting in Damascus: A Study Based on Arabic Manuscripts of Ibn Khaldun's "Autobiography."* Berkeley: University of California Press.

Flint, R. (1893) *History of the Philosophy of History.* Edinburgh

Fromherz, A. J. (2010). *Ibn Khaldun: life and times.* Edinburgh: Edinburgh University Press.

Gellner, E. (1981). *Muslim Society.* Cambridge: Cambridge University Press.

Gilroy, P. (2002). *There Ain't No Black in the Union Jack: The*

*Cultural Politics of Race and Nation* (3rd ed. with new Introduction). London: Routledge.

Gilroy, P. (2004). *After Empire: Melancholia or Convivial Culture?* Abingdon: Routledge.

Goodman, L.E. (2003) *Islamic Humanism*. Oxford: Oxford University Press.

Günther, S. (2006). Be Masters in That You Teach and Continue to Learn: Medieval Muslim Thinkers on Educational Theory. *Comparative Education Review, 50*(3), 367–388.

Hall, S., Critchner, C., Jefferson T., Clarke J., Roberts, B. (1978) *Policing the Crisis: Mugging, the State and Law and Order*. London: Macmillan.

Hannoum, A. (2003). Translation and the Colonial Imaginary: Ibn Khaldûn Orientalist. *History and Theory, 42*(1), 61–81.

Himmich, B. (2009) *The Polymath: A Modern Arabic Novel.* Cairo: American University in Cario.

Hitti, P.K. (1991) *History of the Arabs.* New York: London: Palgrave.

Hillenbrand, R. (1994) *Ornament of the World: Medieval Cordoba as a Cultural Centre.* In Jayyusi, S. The Legacy of Muslim Spain (2 Volumes). Leiden: Brill.

Hodgson, M. (1977) *The Venture of Islam: Conscience and History in World Civilisation.* Chicago: University of Chicago Press.

Irwin, R. (2018). *Ibn Khaldun: an intellectual biography.* Princeton, New Jersey: Princeton University Press.

Jayyusi, S. (1994) *The Legacy of Muslim Spain* (2 Volumes). Leiden: Brill.

Ibn Khaldun (2017) *Shifa al-Sail li-Tahdhib al-Masail* (Yumna Ozer,Trans) London: The Islamic Text Society.

Ibn Khaldun (1958). *The Muqaddimah: An Introduction to History* (F. Rosenthal, Trans. Vol. 1–3). London: Routledge & Kegan Paul.

Ibn Khaldûn, I., Dawood, N. J., Rosenthal, F., & Lawrence, B. B. (2015). *The Muqaddimah: an Introduction to History - Abridged Edition.* Princeton: Princeton University Press.

Ibn Qayyim al-Jawziyya (2016) *Mifta Sar al-Sa'ada (On Knowledge)* (Zeni, T.A. Translator) London: Islamic Text Society.

Ibn Tufail (1982) *The Journey of the Soul: The Story of Hai Ibn Yaqzan.* London: Octagon Press.

Kosei, M. (2002) What Ibn Khaldun Saw in Egypt. *Mamluk Studies Review* (6), 109–131.

Lacoste, Y. (1984). *Ibn Khaldun.* London: Verso.

Lawrence, B. (1997) *Bruce Lawrence and Islamic Ideology.* Leiden: Brill.

Mahdi, M. (1957). *Ibn Khaldun's Philosophy of History: A Study in the Philosophic Foundation of the Science of Culture.* London.

Makdisi, G. (1984) *Rise of Colleges. Institutions of Learning in Islam and the West*. Edinburgh: Edinburgh University Press.

Malešević, S. (2015). Where does group solidarity come from? Gellner and Ibn Khaldun revisited. *Thesis eleven, 128*(1), 85–99.

Marozzi, J. (2004) Tamerlane, Sword of Islam and Conquer of the World. London: De Capo Press.

Mayo L, Miah S. Zombie Disciplines: Knowledge, Anticipatory Imagination, and Becoming in Postnormal Times. *World Futures Review*. 2021;13(2):157–171.

Miah, S. (2015) *Muslim Schooling and the Question of Self Segregation*. London: Palgrave.

Moosa, E. (2015) *What is a Madrasa?* Edinburgh: Edinburgh University Press.

Ozer, Y. (2017) *Ibn Khaldun on Sufism* in Ibn Khaldun (2017) *Shifa al-Sail li-Tahdhib al-Masail* (Yumna Ozer, Trans) London: The Islamic Text Society.

Rabī, M. R. (1967) *The Political Theory of Ibn Khaldūn*. Leiden: E.J. Brill.

Rosenthal, F. (1970) *Knowledge Triumphant: The Concept of Knowledge in Medieval Islam*. Leiden: Brill.

Rumi, J.A. (2008) *The Masnavi* (Translated by Jawed Mujadid 4 volumes) Oxford: Oxford University Press.

Said, E. W. (1979). *Orientalism* (First Vintage Books ed.). New York: Vintage Books.

Sardar, Z. (1998) *Postmodernism and the Other: The New Imperialism of Western Culture*. London: Pluto Press.

Sardar, Z., & Yassin-Kassab, R. (2011). *Critical Muslim: 1, The Arabs are alive* (Vol. 1;1.;). London, [England]: C Hurst & Co (Publishers) Ltd.

Sardar, Z. (2020) The Smog of Ignorance: Knowledge and Wisdom in Postnormal Times. *Futures* 120.

Schmidt, N. (1930). *Ibn Khaldun: Historian, Sociologist and Philosopher*. New York: Columbia University Press.

Schmidt, N. (1926) Manuscripts of Ibn Khaldun, Journal of American Oriental Society, vols X–V1.

Tibawi, A.L. (1972) *Islamic Education: Its Traditions and Modernization into Arab National Systems*. London: Luzac and Company.

Toynbee, A.J. (1934) A Study of History (12 Volumes) Oxford: Oxford University Press.

Watt, W.M, & Cachia, P. (1996) History of Islamic Spain. Edinburgh: Edinburgh University Press.

# *Index*

Toynbee, Arnold J. 112
translation movement 63, 64, 65, 108
Tunis 4, 19, 21, 25, 34, 41, 82

U

ulama 79
Umayyad 12, 15, 33, 45, 63, 79
umran badawi 87, 98
umran hadari 87, 98

W

waqf 26, 27

Y

Yemen 4, 12, 14, 19

Z

Zahirite 18
Zoroastrianism 110

Milton Keynes UK
Ingram Content Group UK Ltd.
UKHW010615050124
435507UK00002B/8

9 781915 025395